TIGHTCORNERED

TIGHTCORNERED

by Ken Grundy & Malcolm Willett

Andrews and McMeel
A Universal Press Syndicate Company
Kansas City

Tight Corner is distributed internationally by Universal Press Syndicate.

ISBN: 0-8362-2124-9

Library of Congress Catalog Card Number: 96-84109

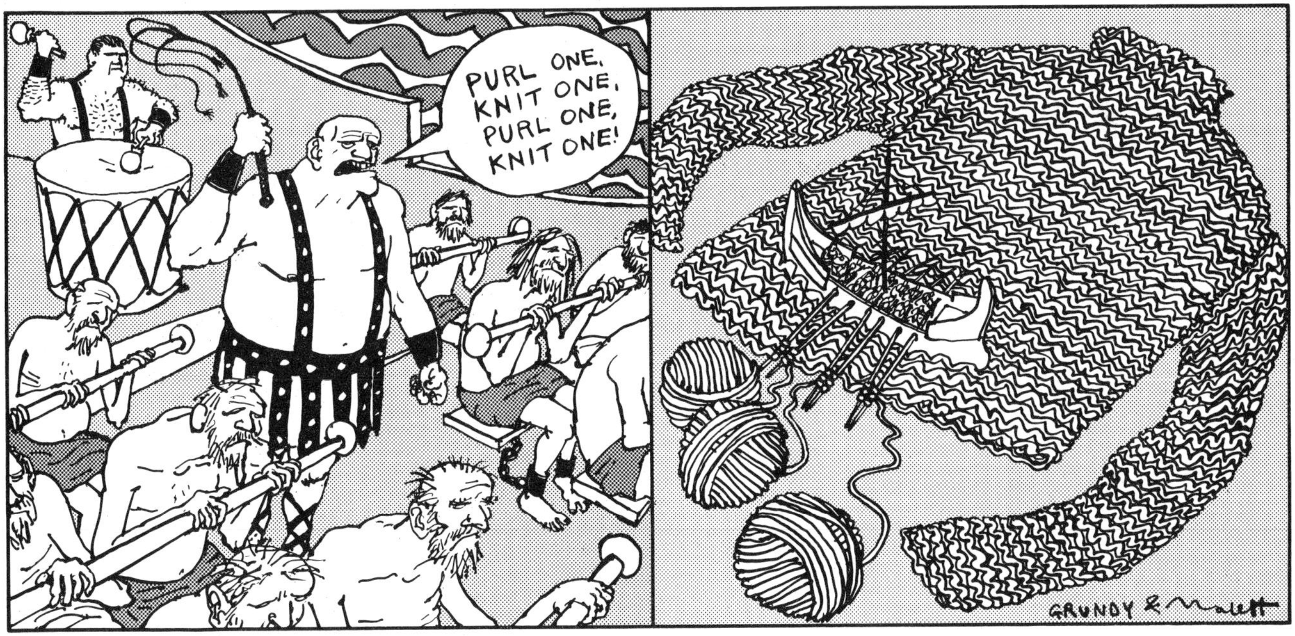
PURL ONE, KNIT ONE, PURL ONE, KNIT ONE!
GRUNDY & Mallett

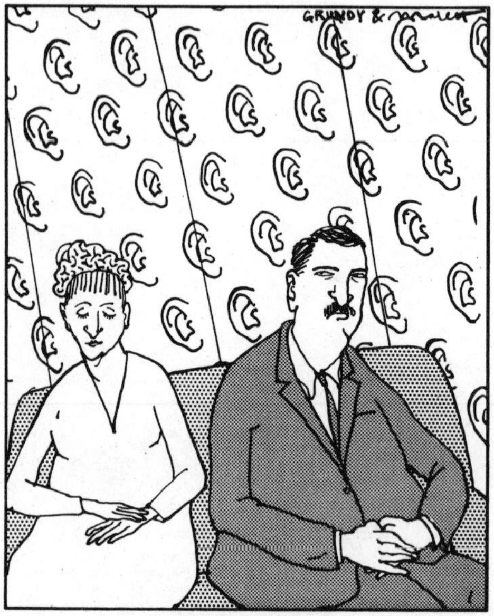
GRUNDY & MALETT

Standard-issue wallpaper
for CIA agents.

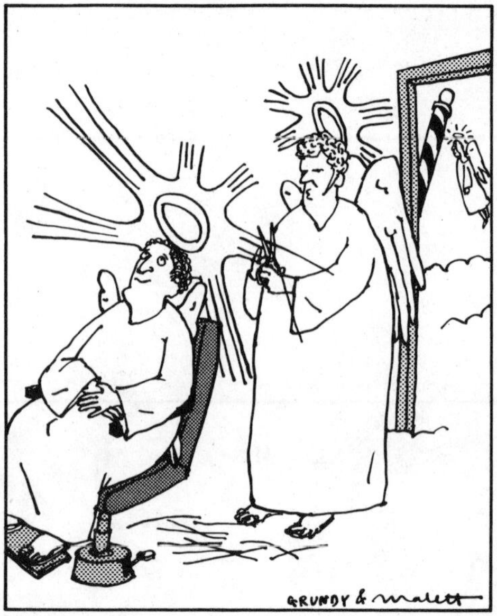
GRUNDY & MALETT

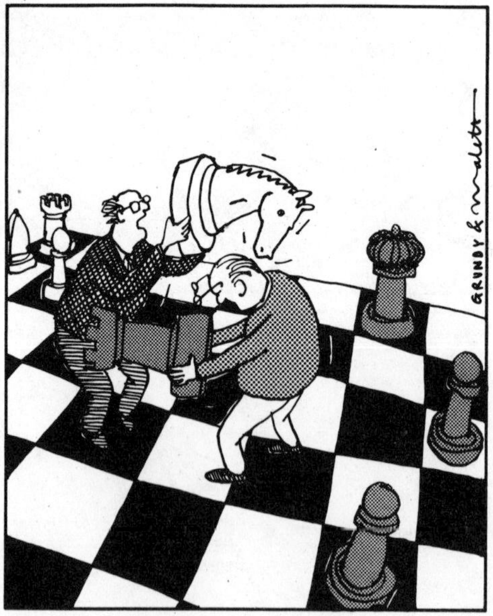
GRUNDY & MALETT

The art of combat chess.

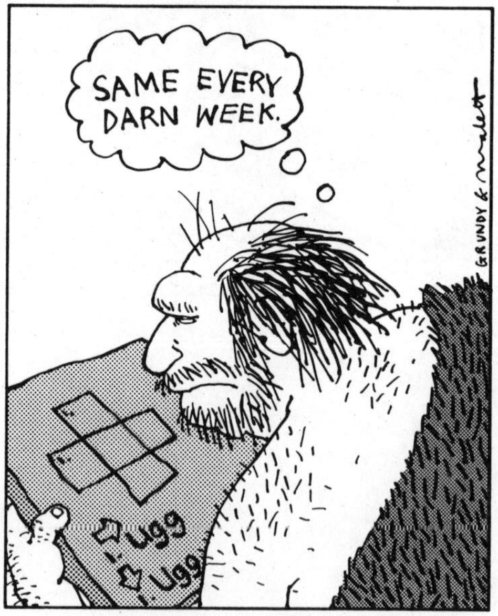
SAME EVERY
DARN WEEK.
GRUNDY & MALETT
UGG
UGG

Early crossword puzzle.

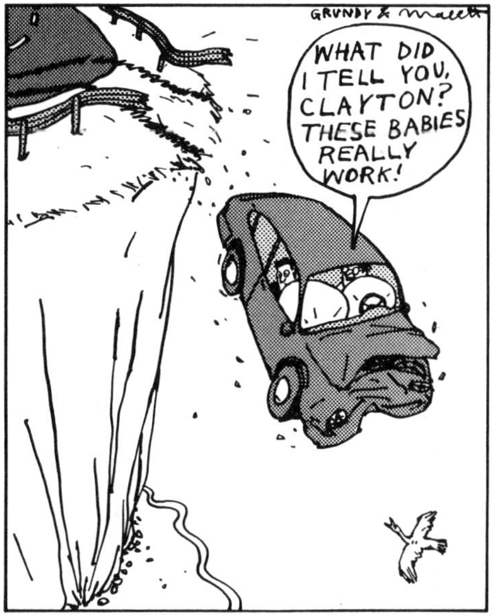
GRUNDY & MALLETT
WHAT DID I TELL YOU, CLAYTON? THESE BABIES REALLY WORK!

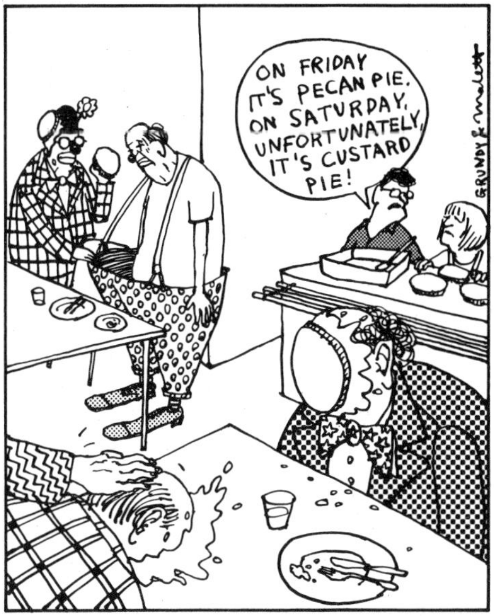
ON FRIDAY IT'S PECAN PIE. ON SATURDAY, UNFORTUNATELY, IT'S CUSTARD PIE!
GRUNDY & MALLETT
At the home for retired clowns.

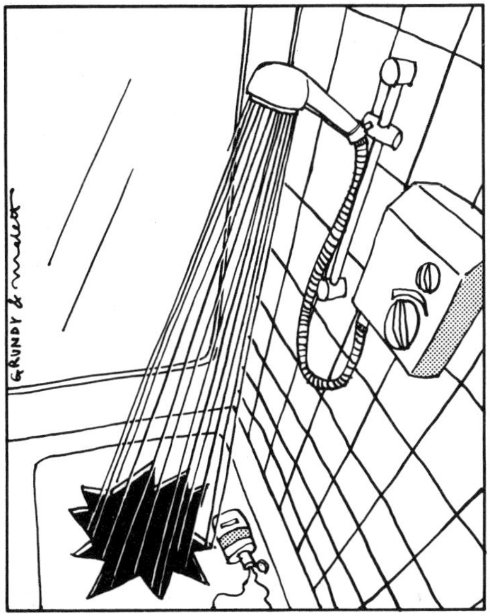
GRUNDY & MALLETT
Power shower.

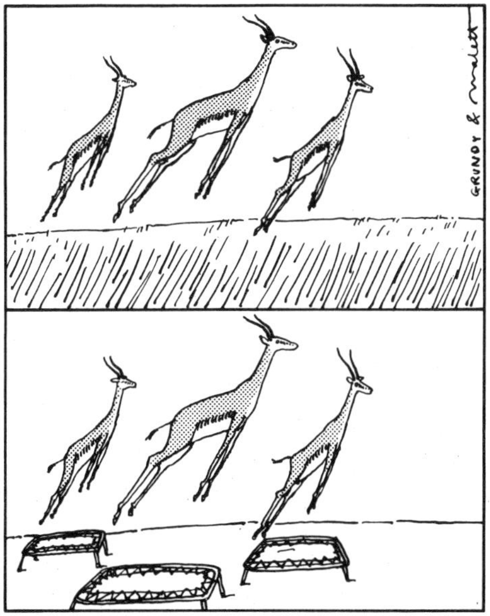
GRUNDY & MALLETT
Revealed: how gazelles manage it.

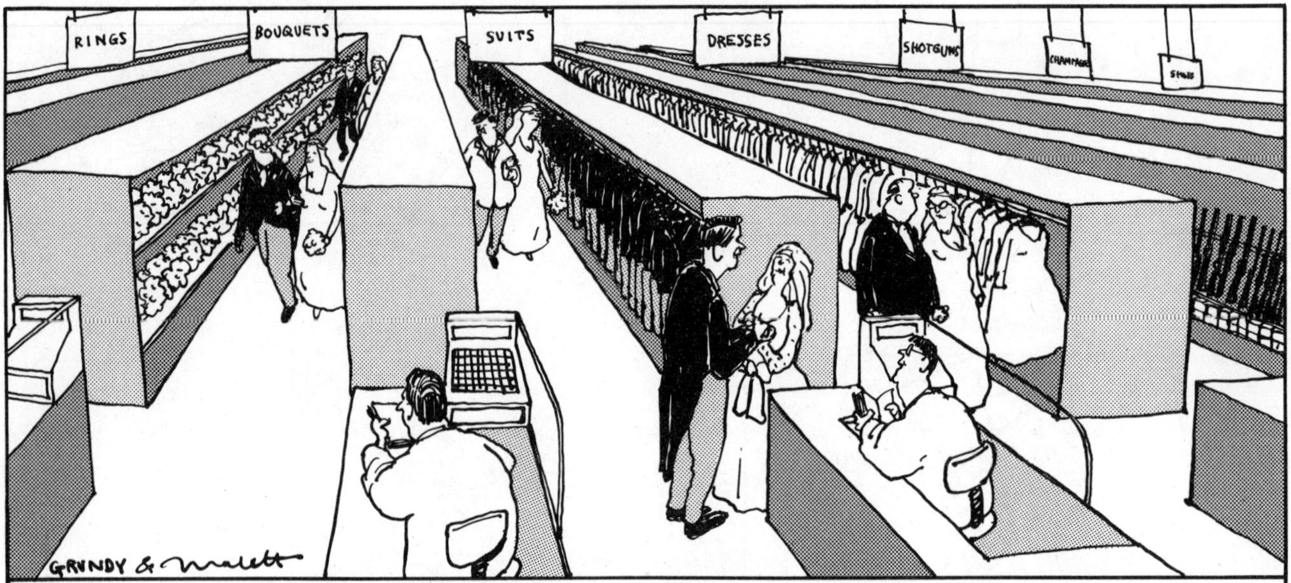
RINGS
BOUQUETS
SUITS
DRESSES
SHOTGUNS

Going down the aisle at the wedding mart.

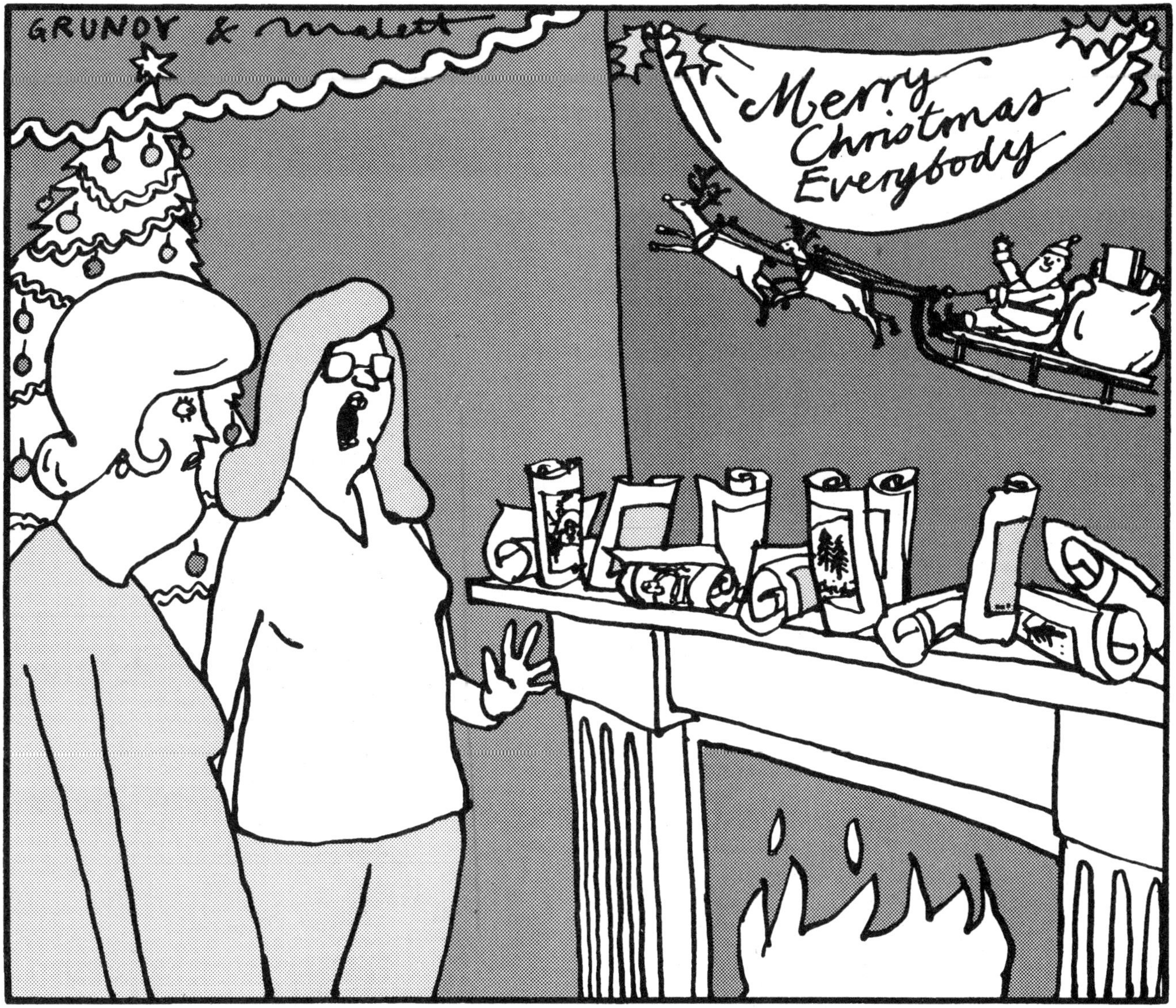
GRUNDY & Malett
Merry Christmas Everybody

"This year, everyone sent a fax."

TO TOWN
WANDERING
STAMPEDING

"What's it to be, Melvin, fast or slow?"

ARTIFICIAL
LIMBS

"Atkins, make that life line a little longer."

"OK, guys, you got me. I shot him while he was asleep."

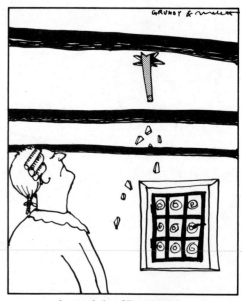

Long John Silver made a very bad roofer.

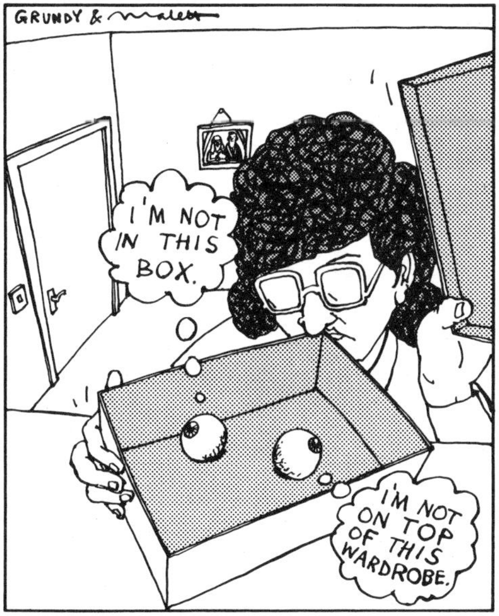
I'M NOT IN THIS BOX.
I'M NOT ON TOP OF THIS WARDROBE.

Pete couldn't hide his lying eyes.

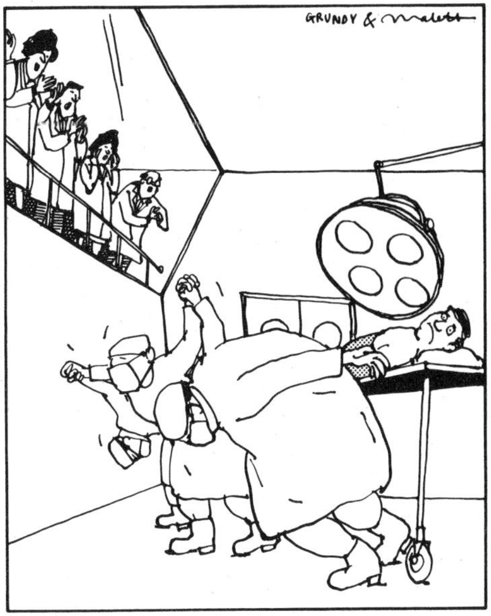

"Encore! . . . Encore!"

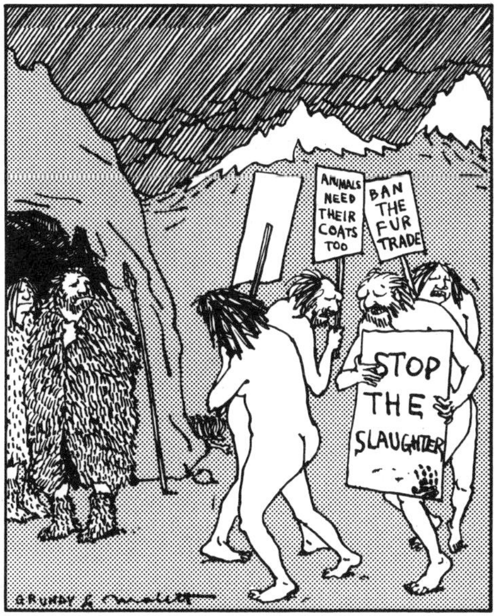
ANIMALS NEED THEIR COATS TOO
BAN THE FUR TRADE
STOP THE SLAUGHTER

6,000 B.C.: the first anti-fur demonstration.

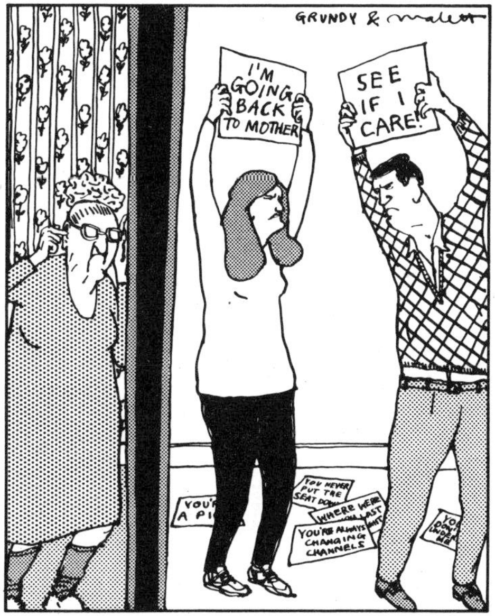
I'M GOING BACK TO MOTHER
SEE IF I CARE!
YOU NEVER PUT THE SEAT DOWN
YOU'RE ALWAYS CHANGING CHANNELS

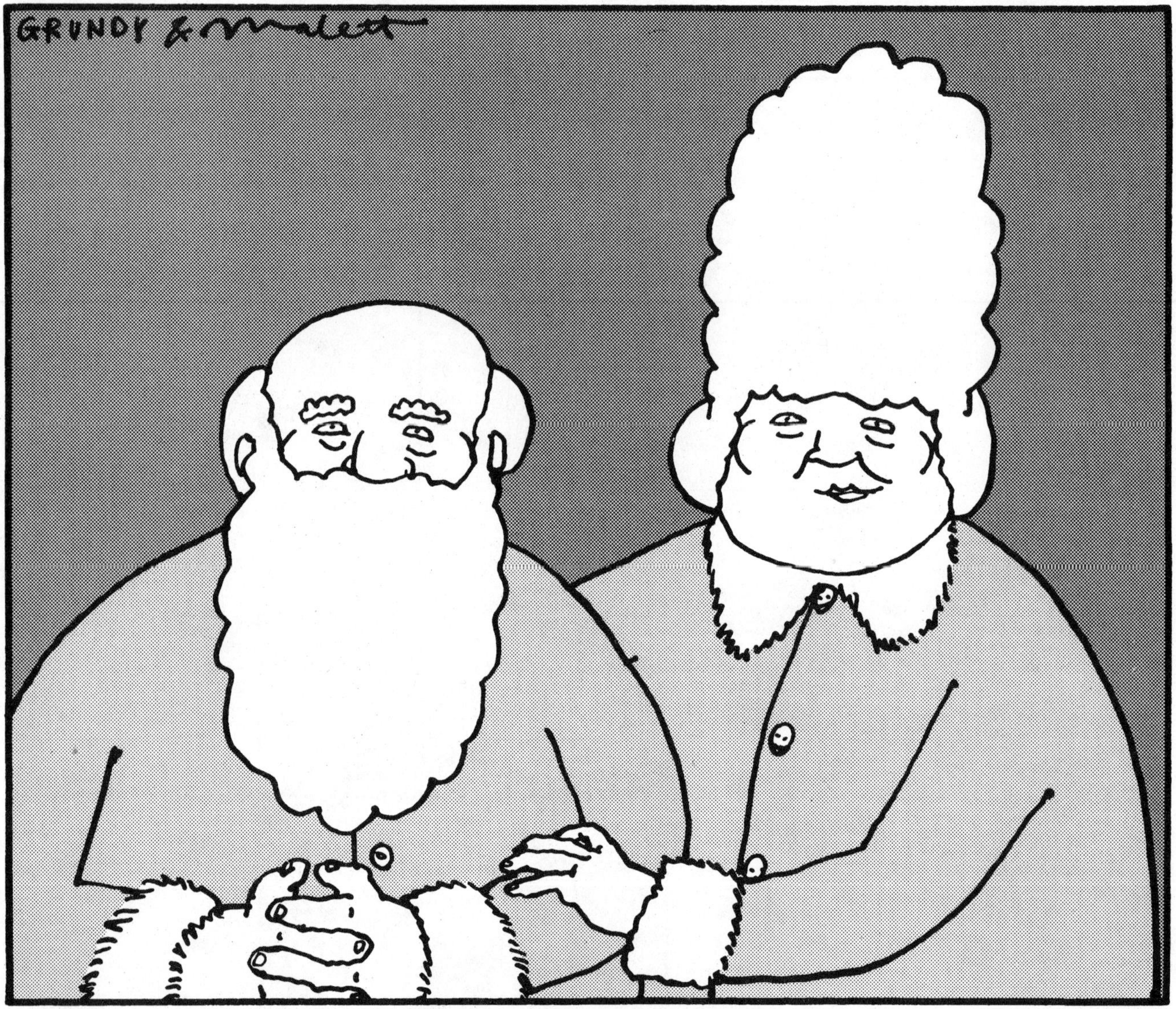
GRUNDY & Malett

Mr. & Mrs. S. Claus.

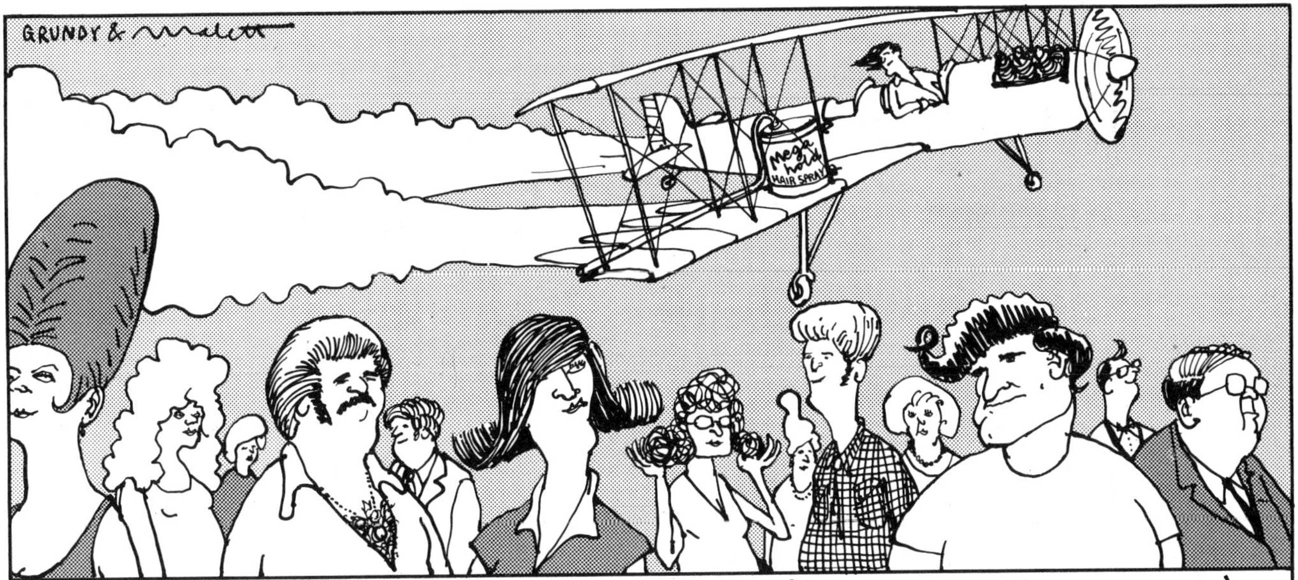
GRUNDY &
Mega hold
HAIR SPRAY

Marcel's job on Friday nights made a change from the usual crop-spraying.

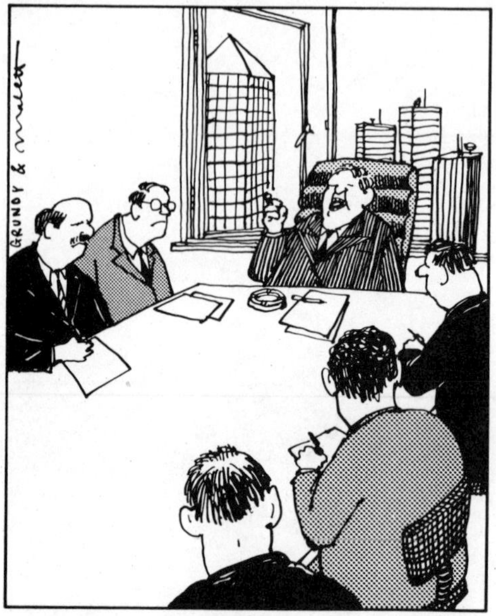
GRUNDY & Malett

"Anyone in disagreement please signify by leaving through the window."

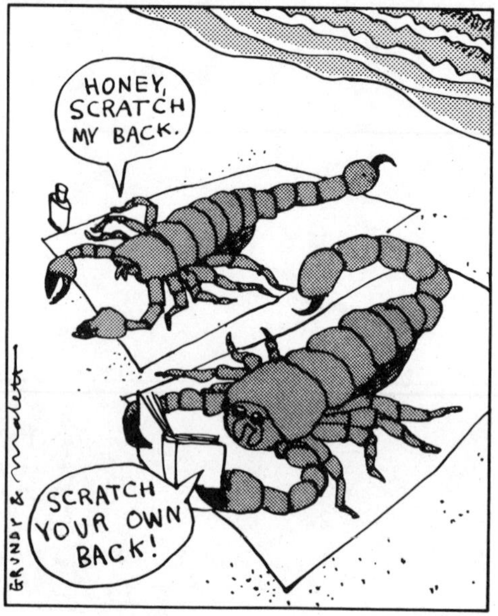
HONEY, SCRATCH MY BACK.
SCRATCH YOUR OWN BACK!
GRUNDY & Malett

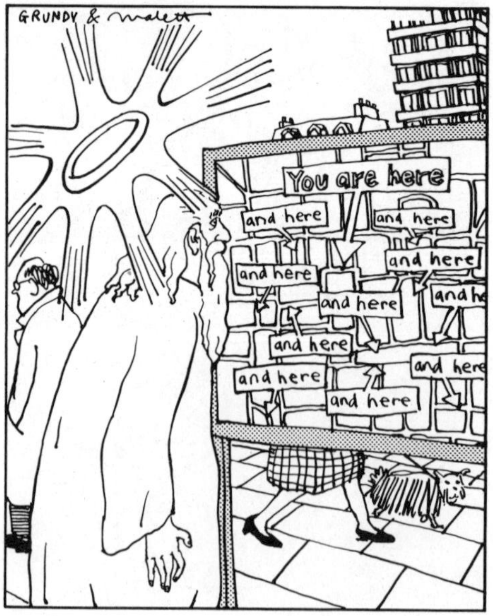
GRUNDY & Malett
You are here
and here
and here
and here
and here
and here
and he
and here
and here
and here
and here

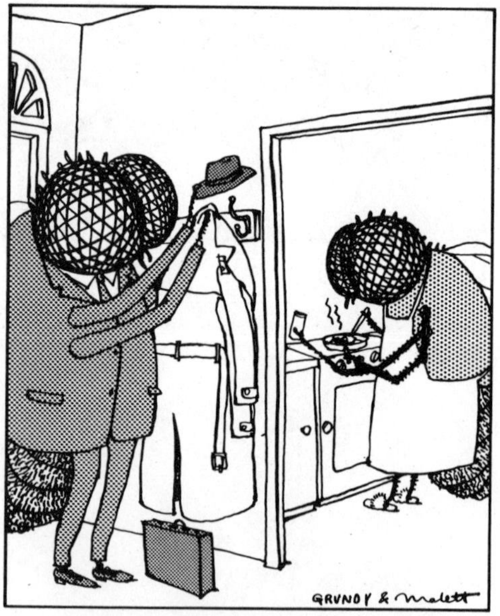
GRUNDY & Malett

"Mmmm, that smells bad! Honey, what's for dinner?"

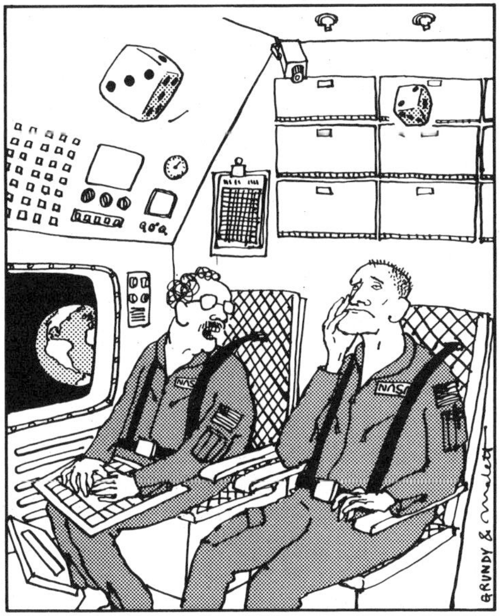
GRUNDY & Malett

"It's no use, Chet. You threw those dice half an hour ago. Let's play something else."

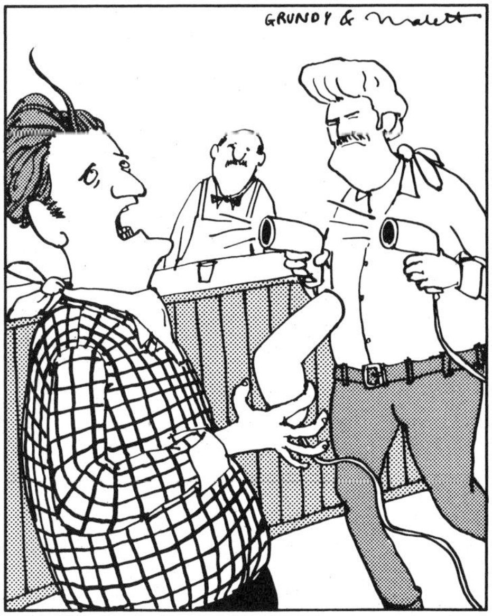
GRUNDY & Malett

Hairdressers of the Wild West.

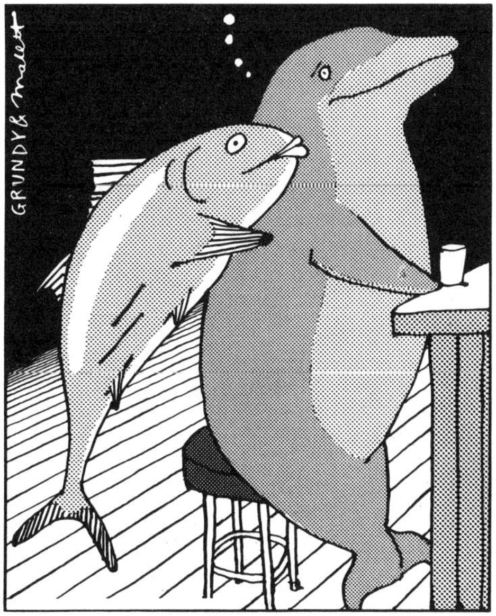
GRUNDY & Malett

Dolphin-*very*-friendly tuna.

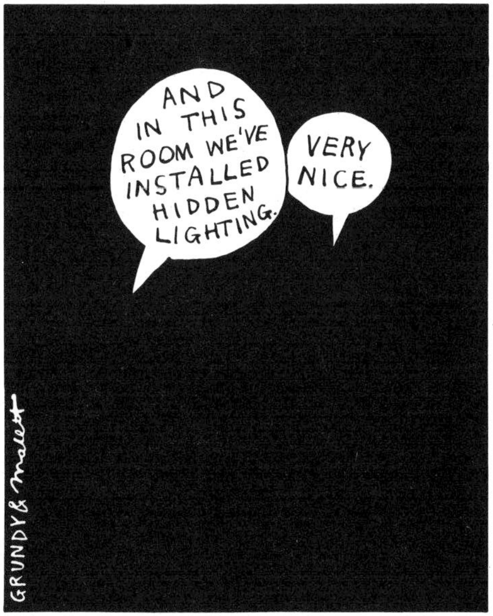
AND IN THIS ROOM WE'VE INSTALLED HIDDEN LIGHTING.
VERY NICE.
GRUNDY & Malett

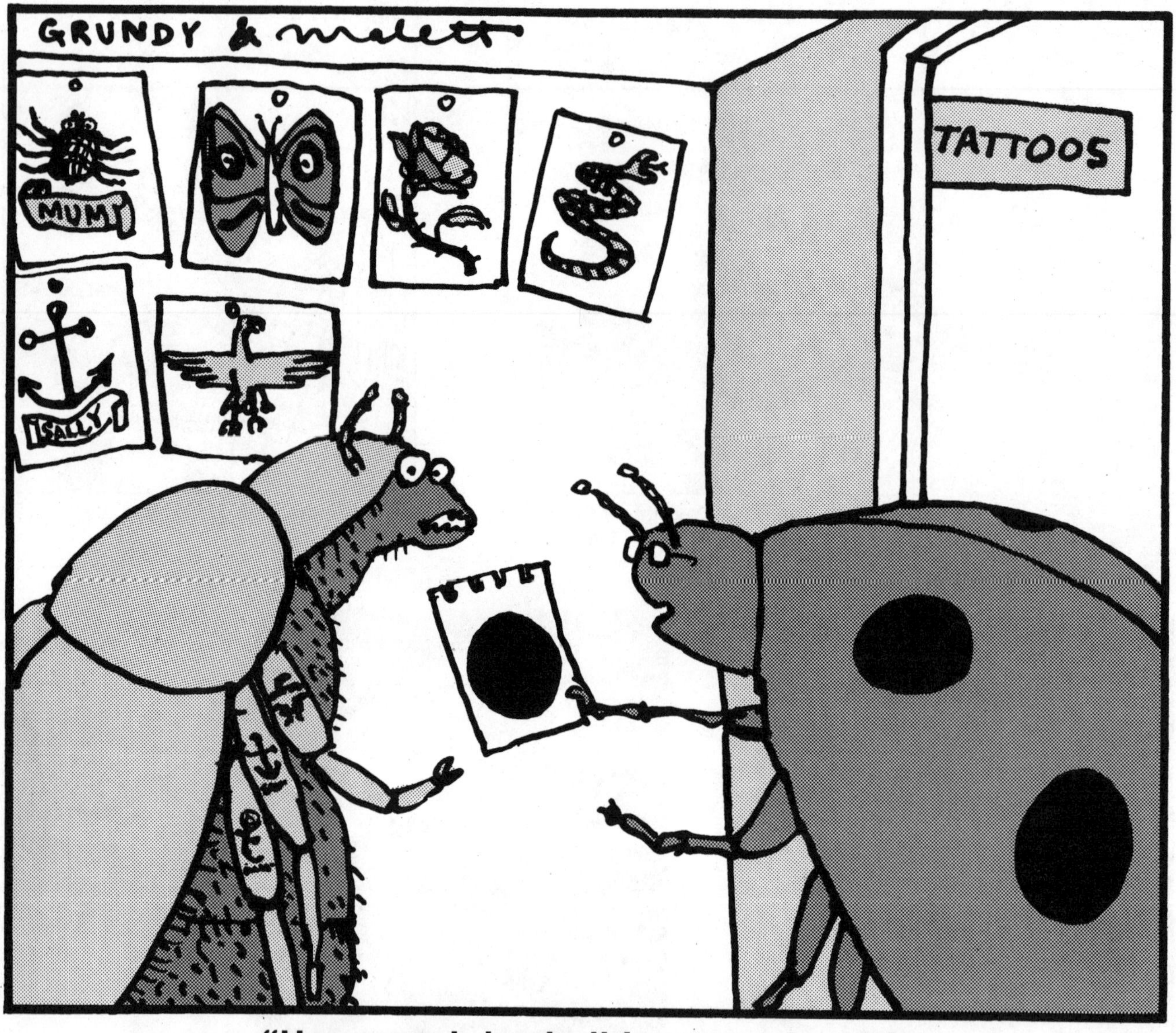
GRUNDY & Malett
MUM
SALLY
TATTOOS

"How much to do this on my back?
It's my own design."

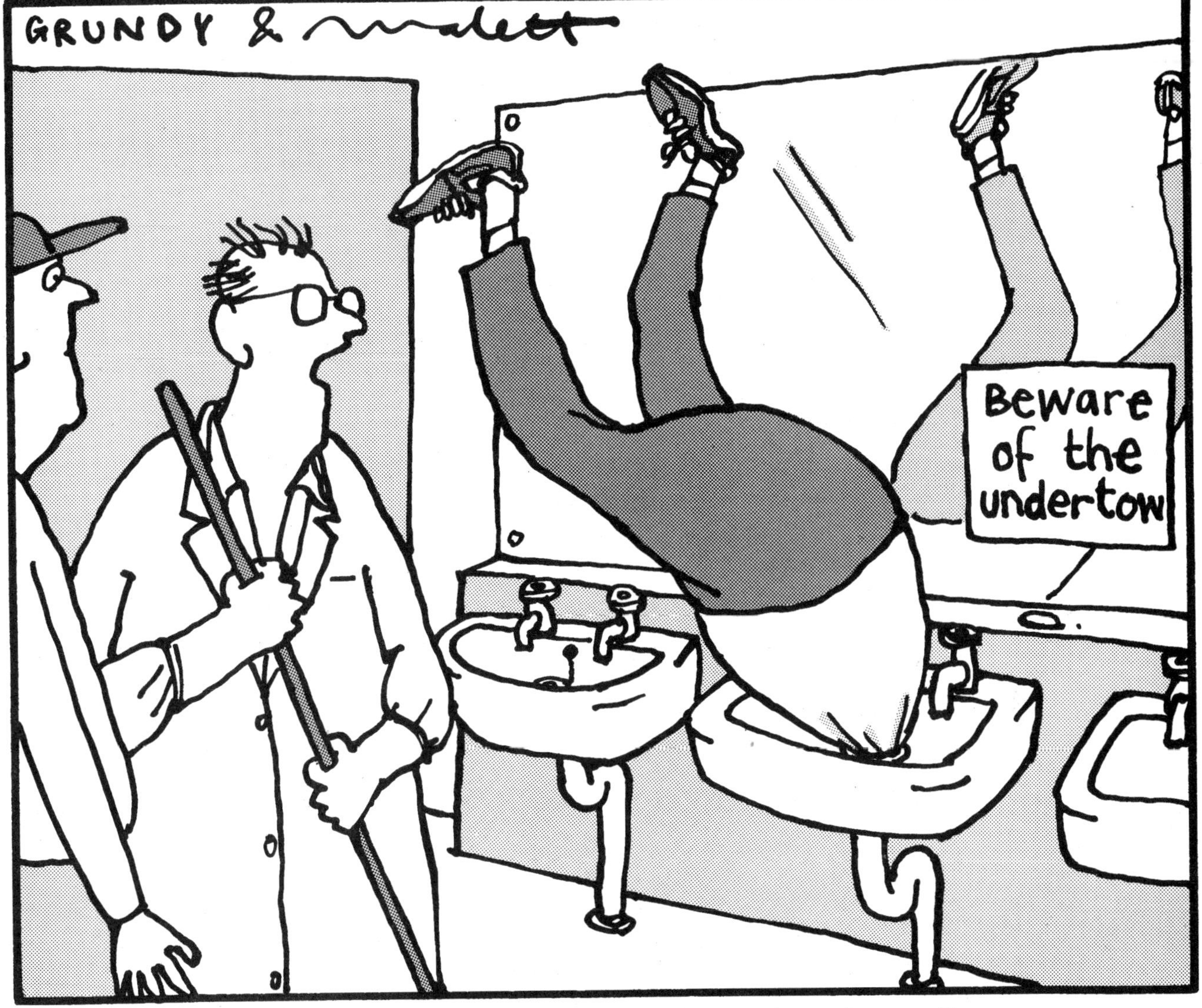
GRUNDY & MALETT
Beware of the undertow

"There's always some guy who doesn't bother to read the sign."

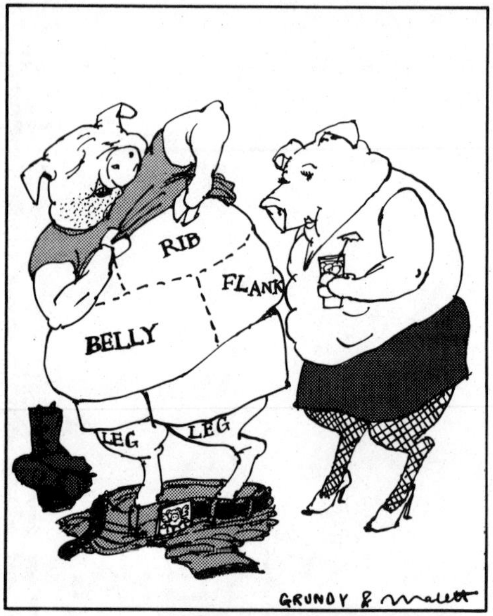
RIB
FLANK
BELLY
LEG
LEG
GRUNDY & Malett
". . . and I had this tattoo
done in Vegas."

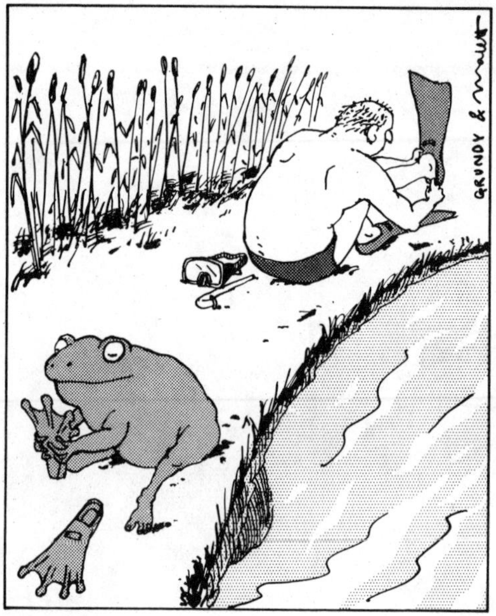
GRUNDY & Malett

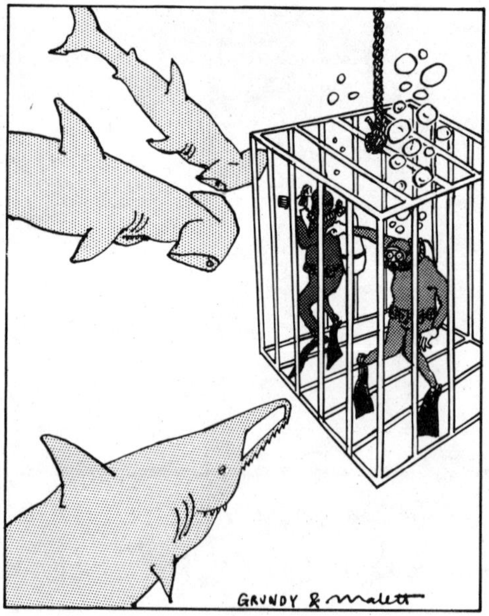
GRUNDY & Malett

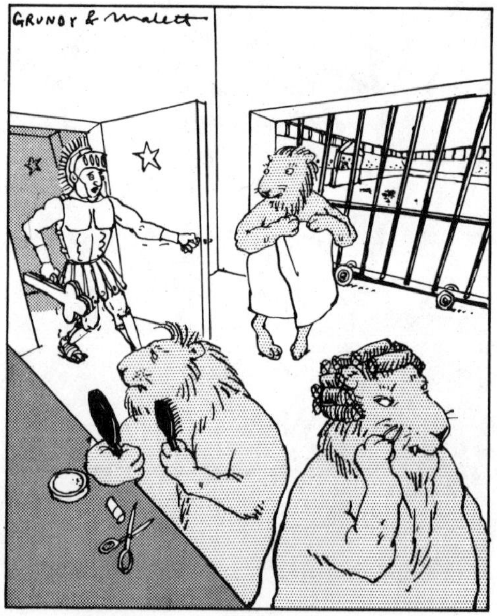
GRUNDY & Malett
"Sorry, wrong dressing room."

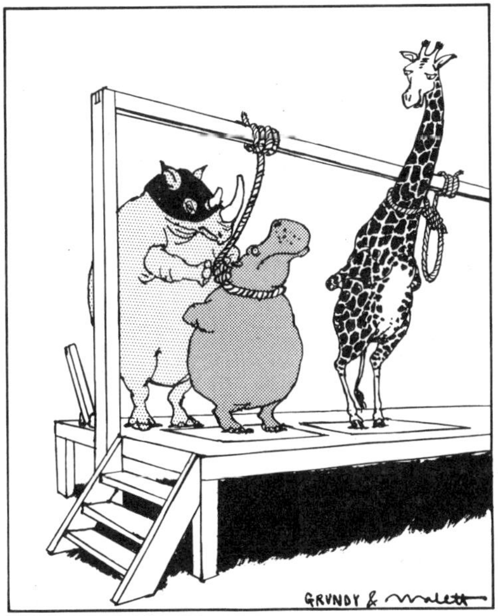

"Appeal? I didn't bother."

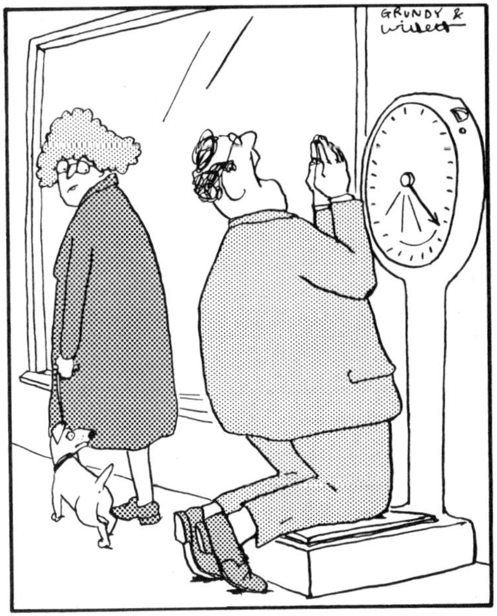

"It works!"

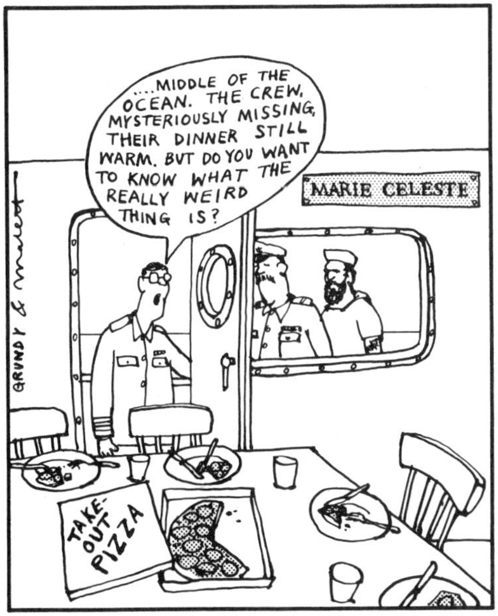
....MIDDLE OF THE OCEAN. THE CREW, MYSTERIOUSLY MISSING, THEIR DINNER STILL WARM. BUT DO YOU WANT TO KNOW WHAT THE REALLY WEIRD THING IS?
MARIE CELESTE
TAKE-OUT PIZZA

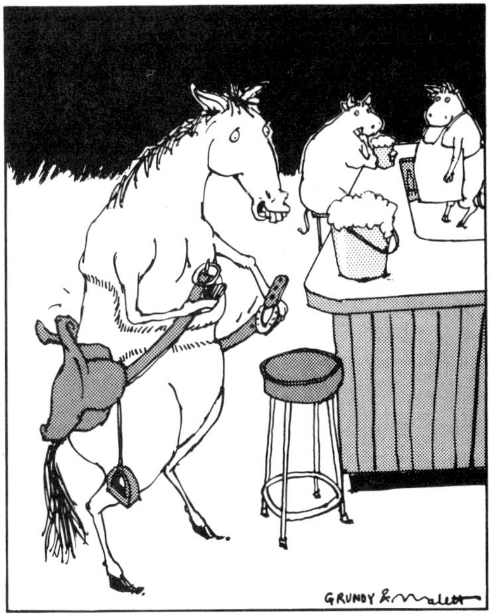

"Oh, boy, does that feel *good*!"

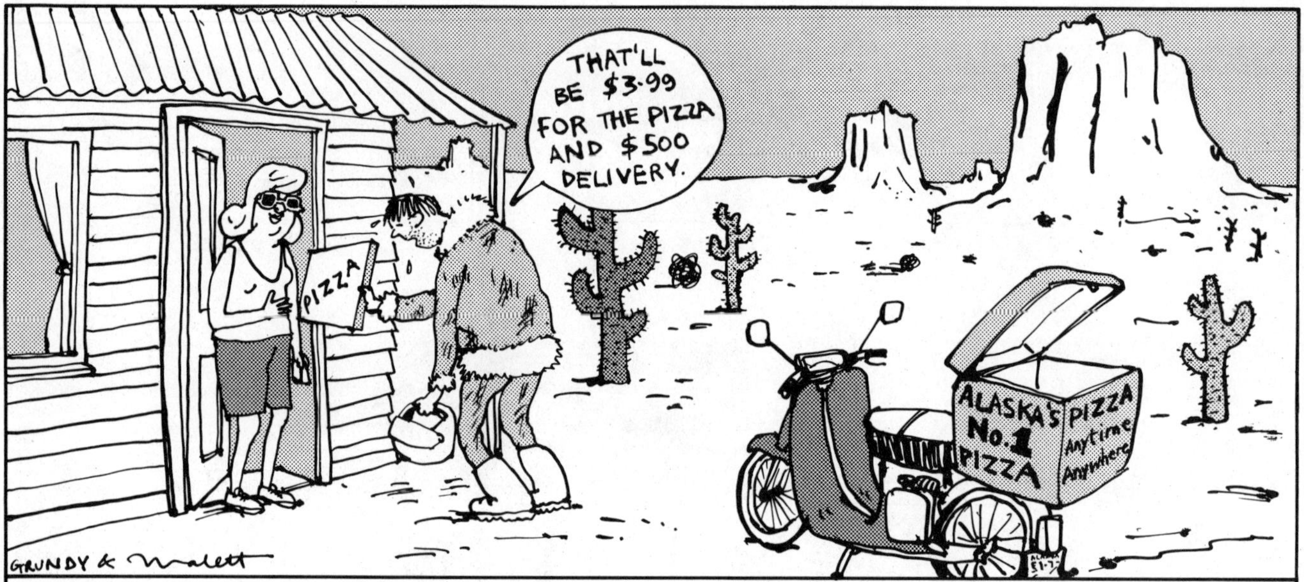
THAT'LL BE $3.99 FOR THE PIZZA AND $500 DELIVERY.
PIZZA
ALASKA'S No.1 PIZZA
PIZZA Anytime Anywhere
GRUNDY & Malett

Bertha had expensive eating habits.

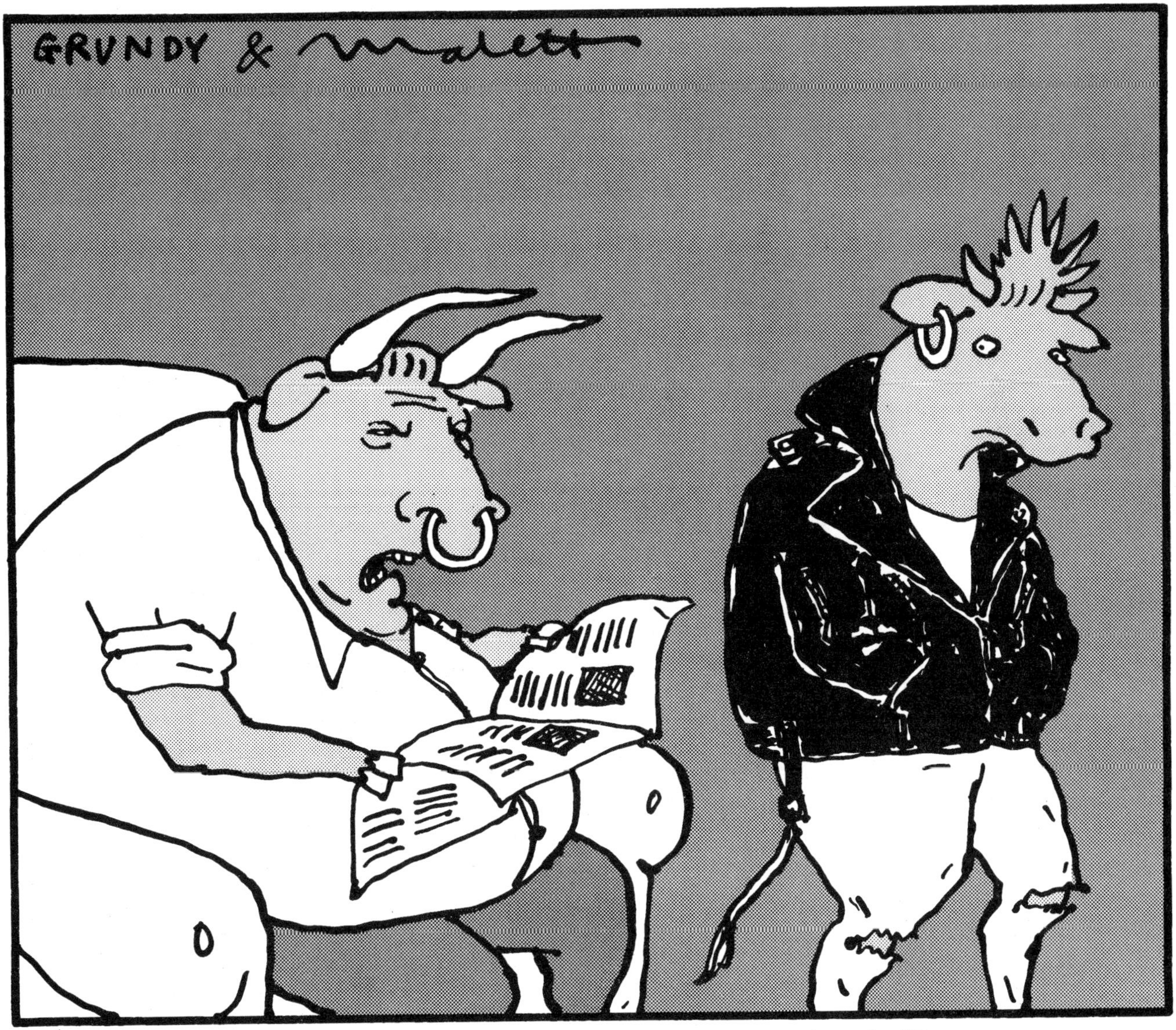
GRUNDY & Malett

". . . and what do you think you look like with that thing in your ear!"

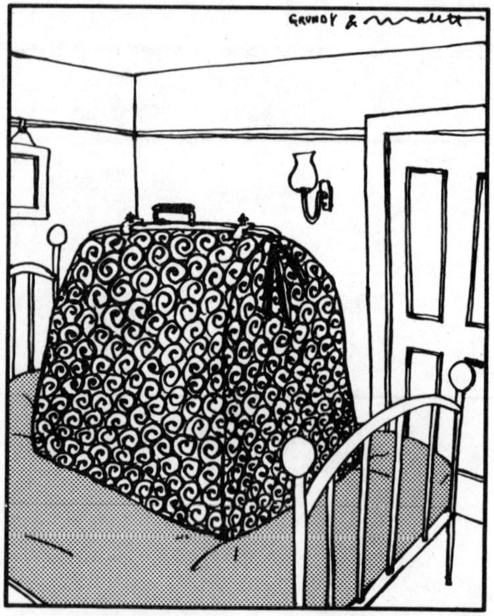
GRUNDY & Malett

Rip Van Winkle's overnight bag.

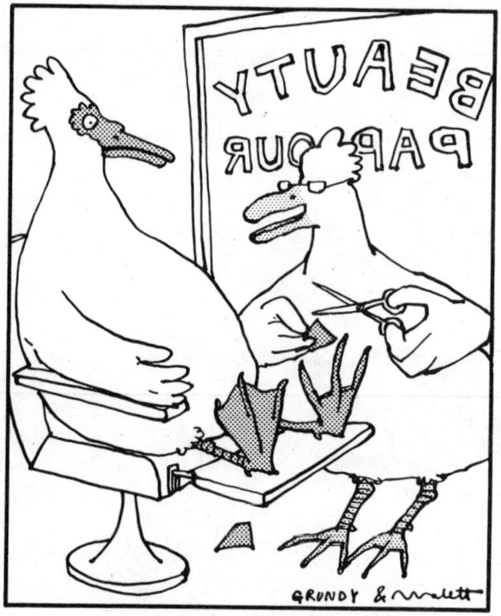
BEAUTY
PARLOUR
GRUNDY & Malett

"You'll swim slower, but, honey, it looks so much better!"

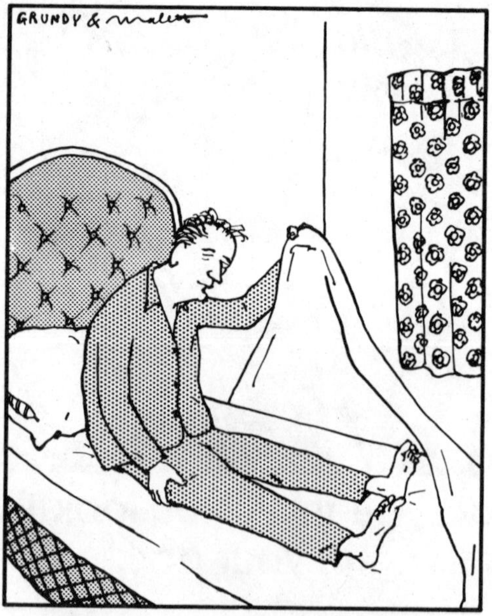
GRUNDY & Malett

After spending hundreds of dollars having acupuncture, Joe woke up with pins and needles one night and cured himself.

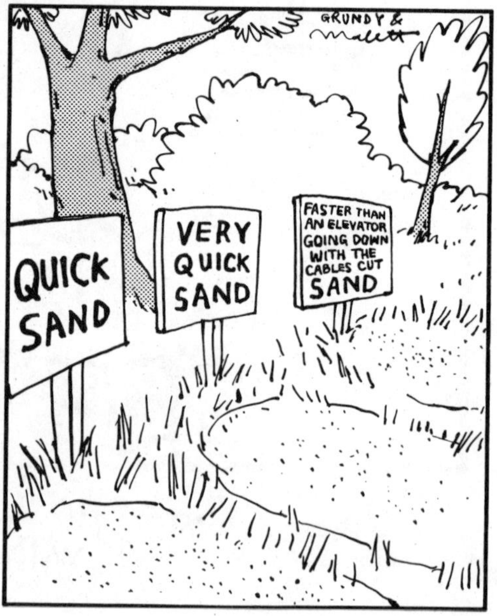
GRUNDY & Malett
QUICK SAND
VERY QUICK SAND
FASTER THAN AN ELEVATOR GOING DOWN WITH THE CABLES CUT SAND

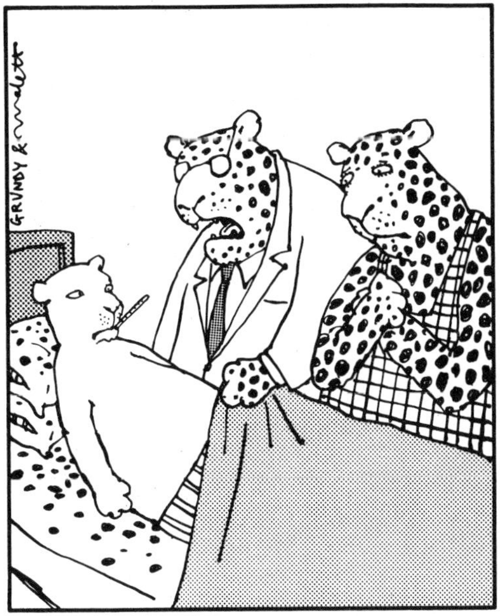
GRUNDY & malett

"I'm afraid it's measles."

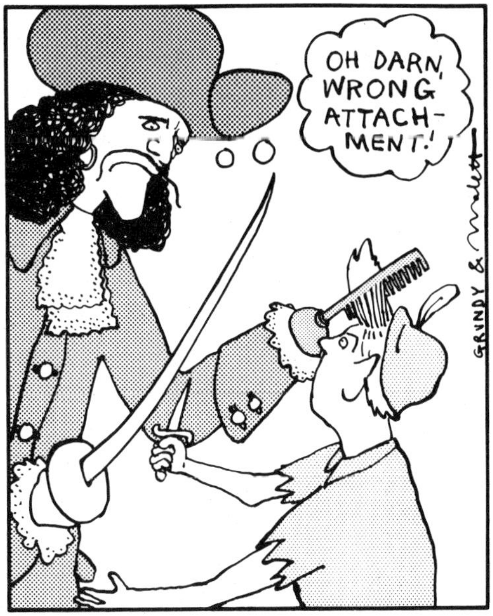
OH DARN, WRONG ATTACH- MENT!
GRUNDY & malett

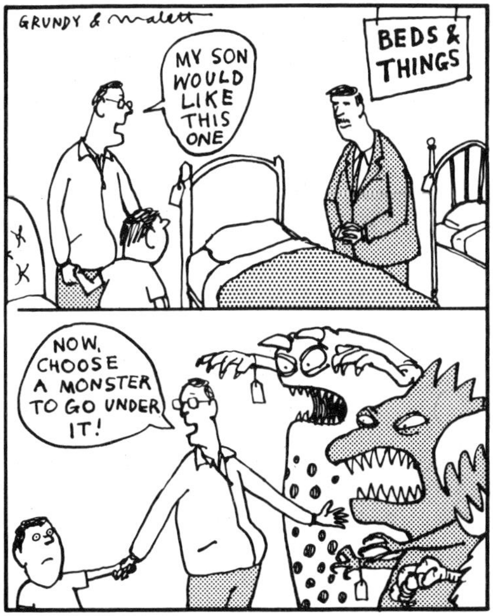
GRUNDY & malett
BEDS & THINGS
MY SON WOULD LIKE THIS ONE
NOW, CHOOSE A MONSTER TO GO UNDER IT!

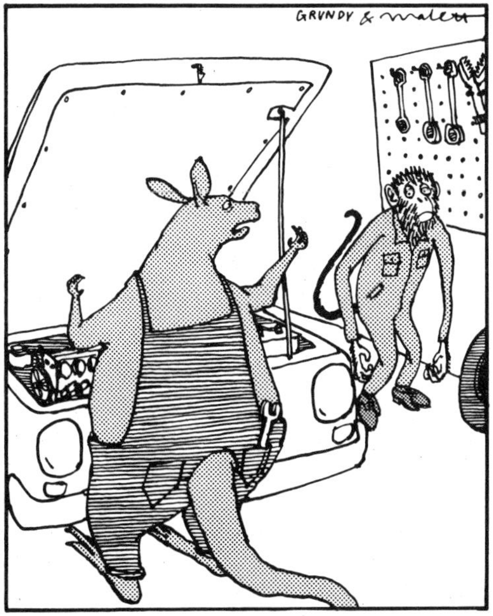
GRUNDY & malett

"Hand me that monk . . . uh . . . wrench."

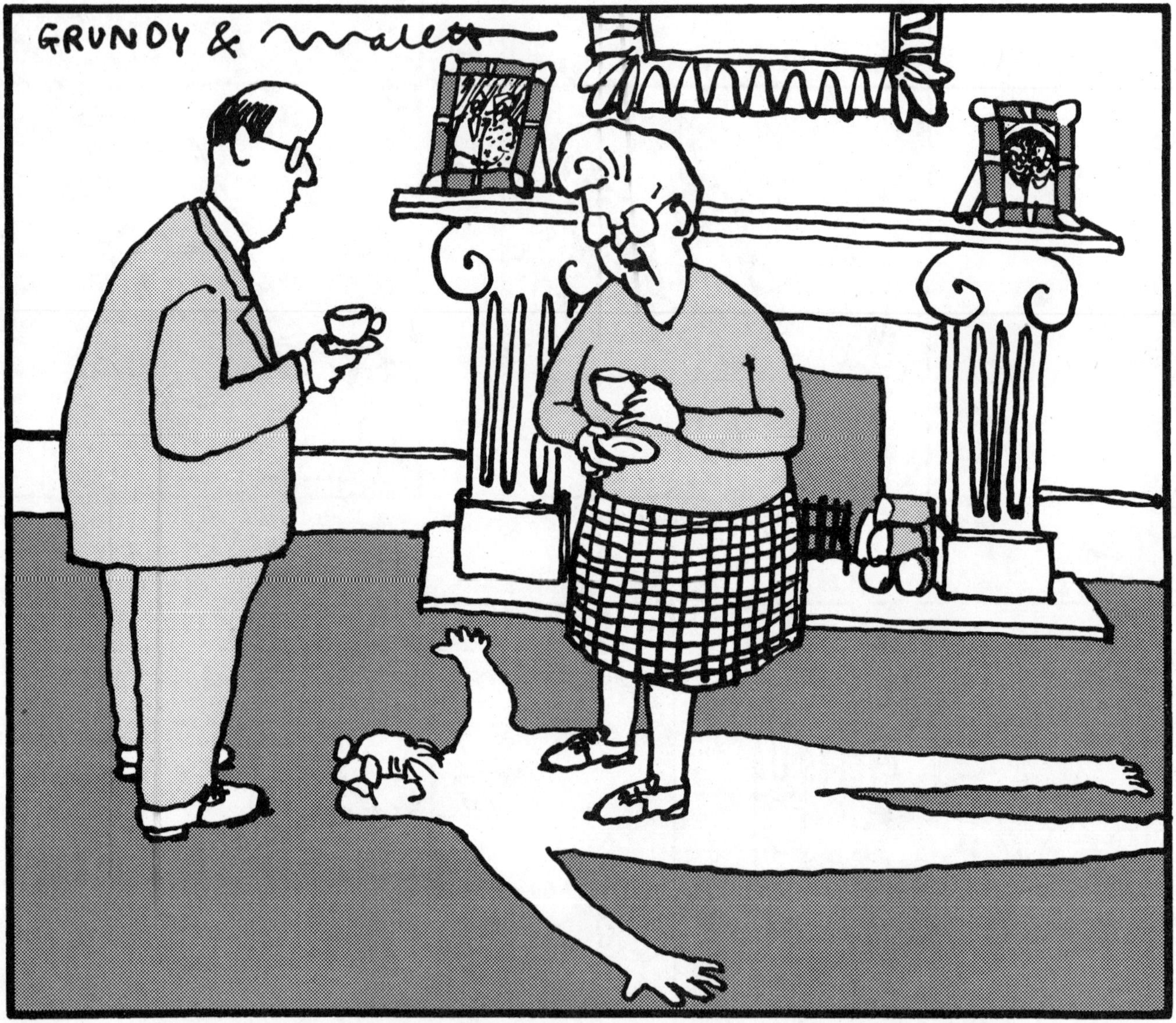
GRUNDY & mallett

"After he retired, he was always under my feet. So when he died, I had him turned into a rug."

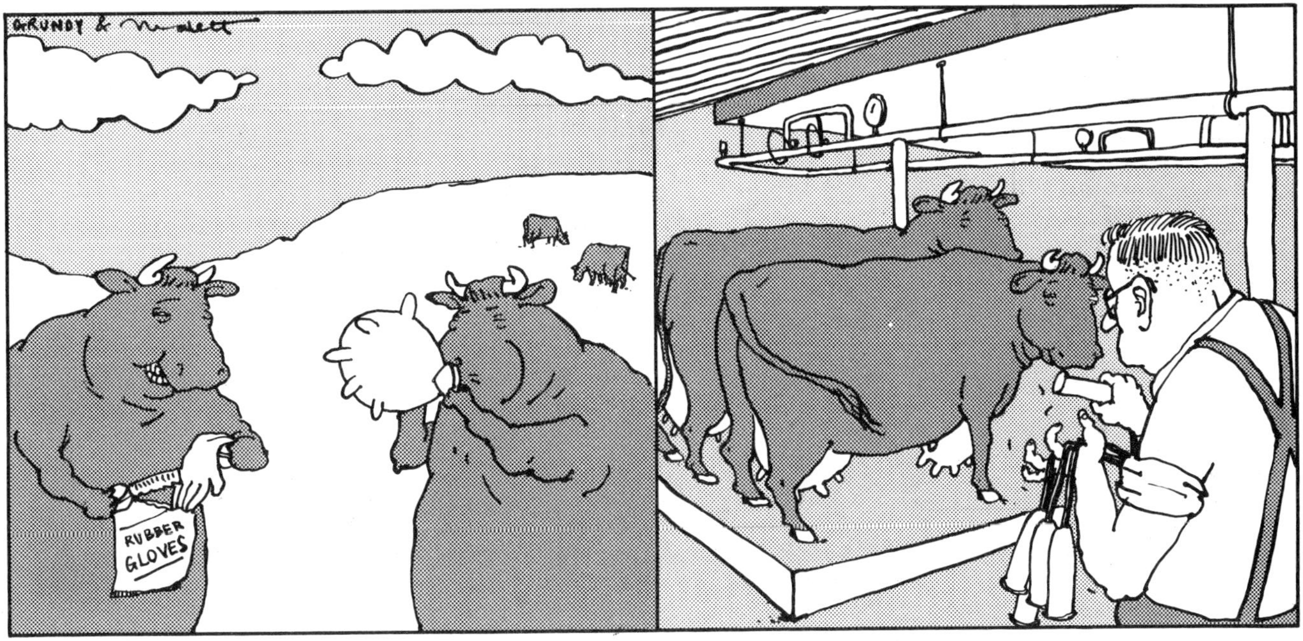
GRUNDY &
RUBBER GLOVES

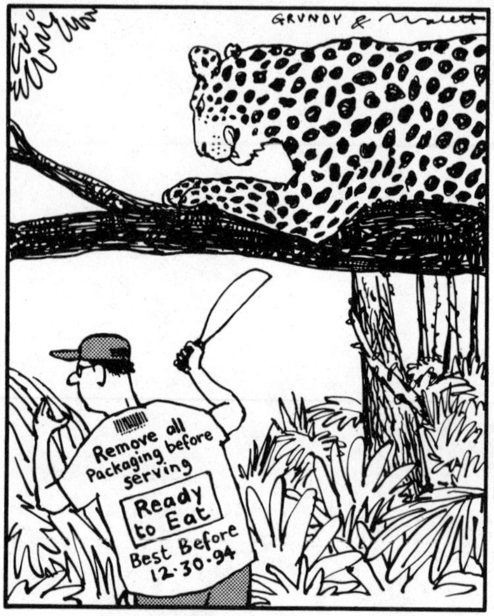
Remove all Packaging before serving
Ready to Eat
Best Before 12-30-94

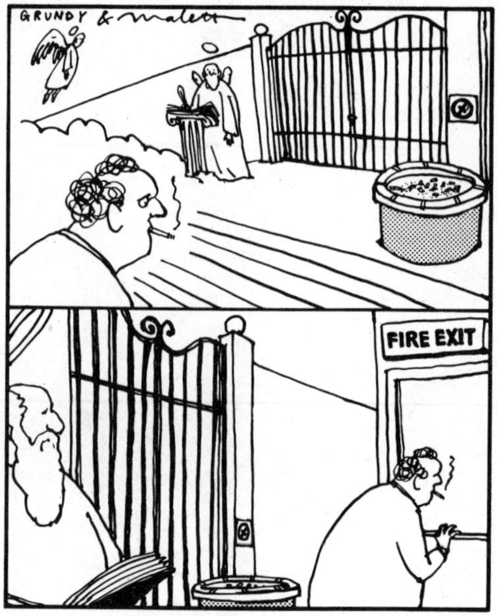
FIRE EXIT

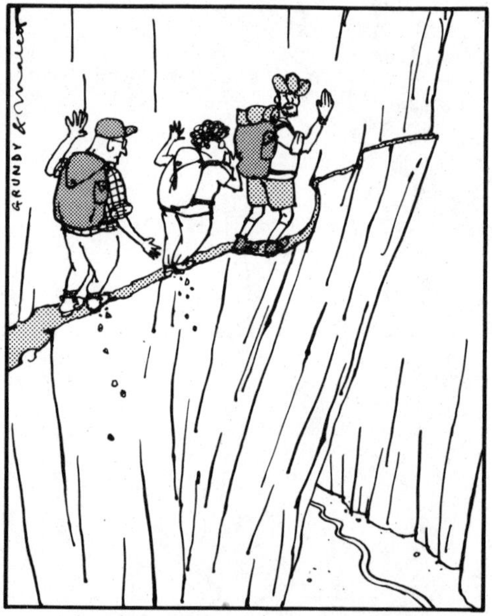

"Don't wander from the path."

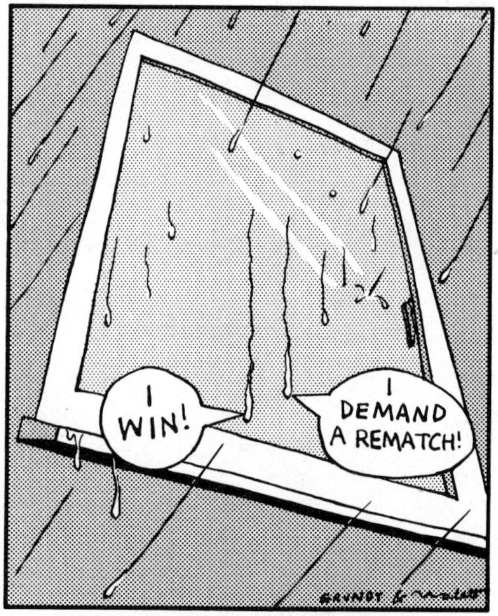
I WIN!
I DEMAND A REMATCH!

Unfortunately, for raindrops there is no second chance.

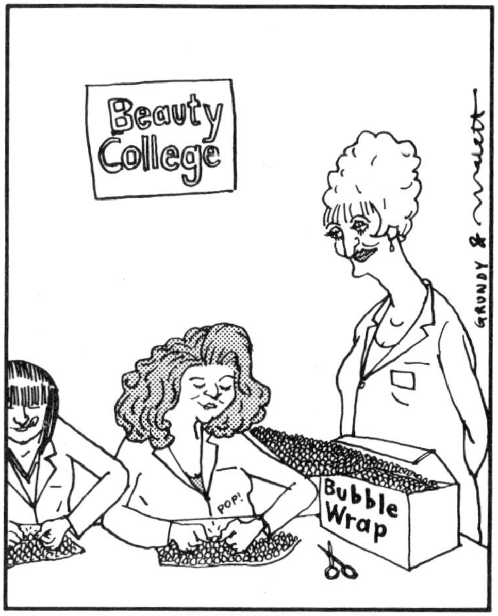
Beauty College
POP!
Bubble Wrap
GRUNDY & Malett

Blackhead-squeezing practice.

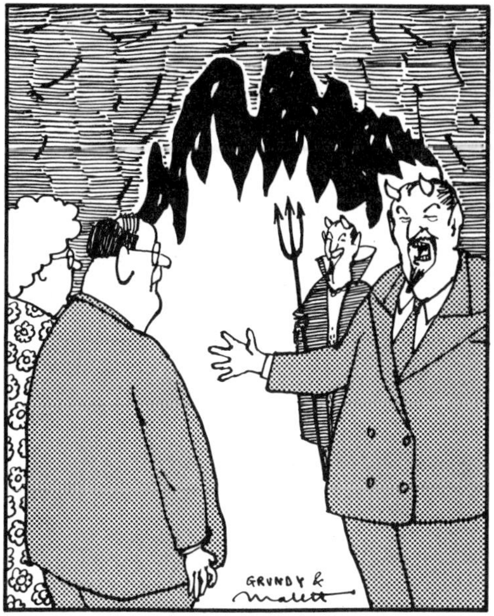
GRUNDY & Malett

"May I wish you all a warm, warm welcome."

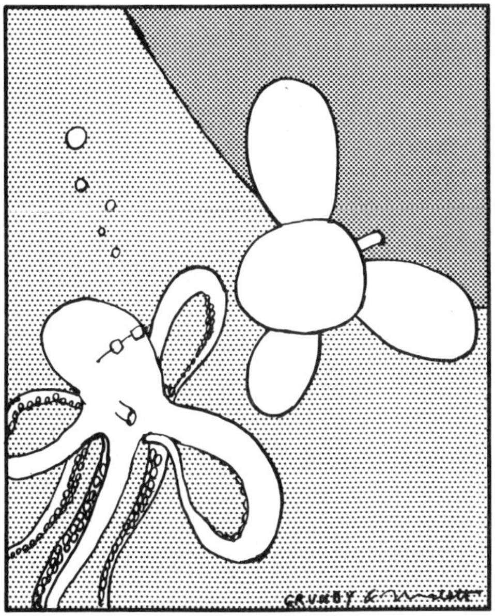

"Hey, babe!"

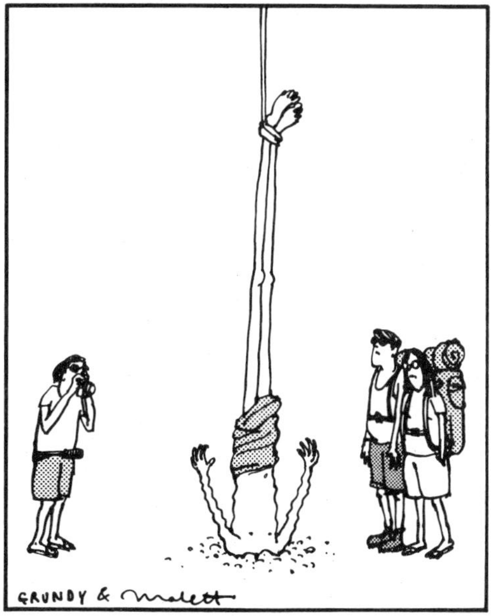
GRUNDY & Malett

Fatal bungee jump for the Indian rubber man.

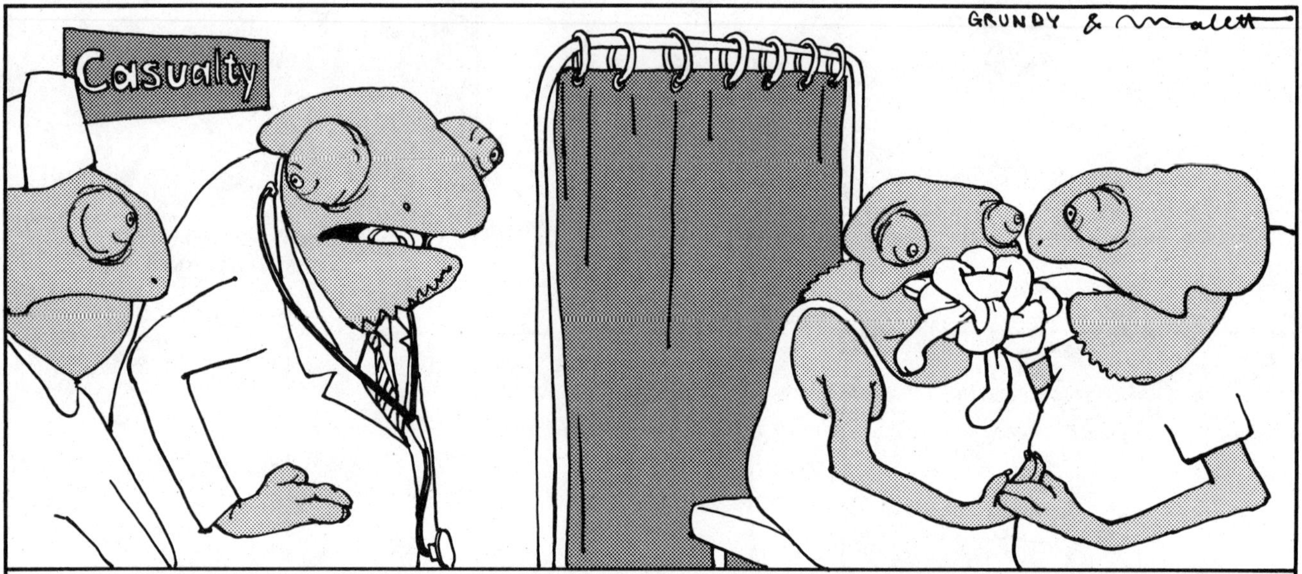
GRUNDY & Malett
Casualty

"Don't these teen-agers know the dangers of French kissing?"

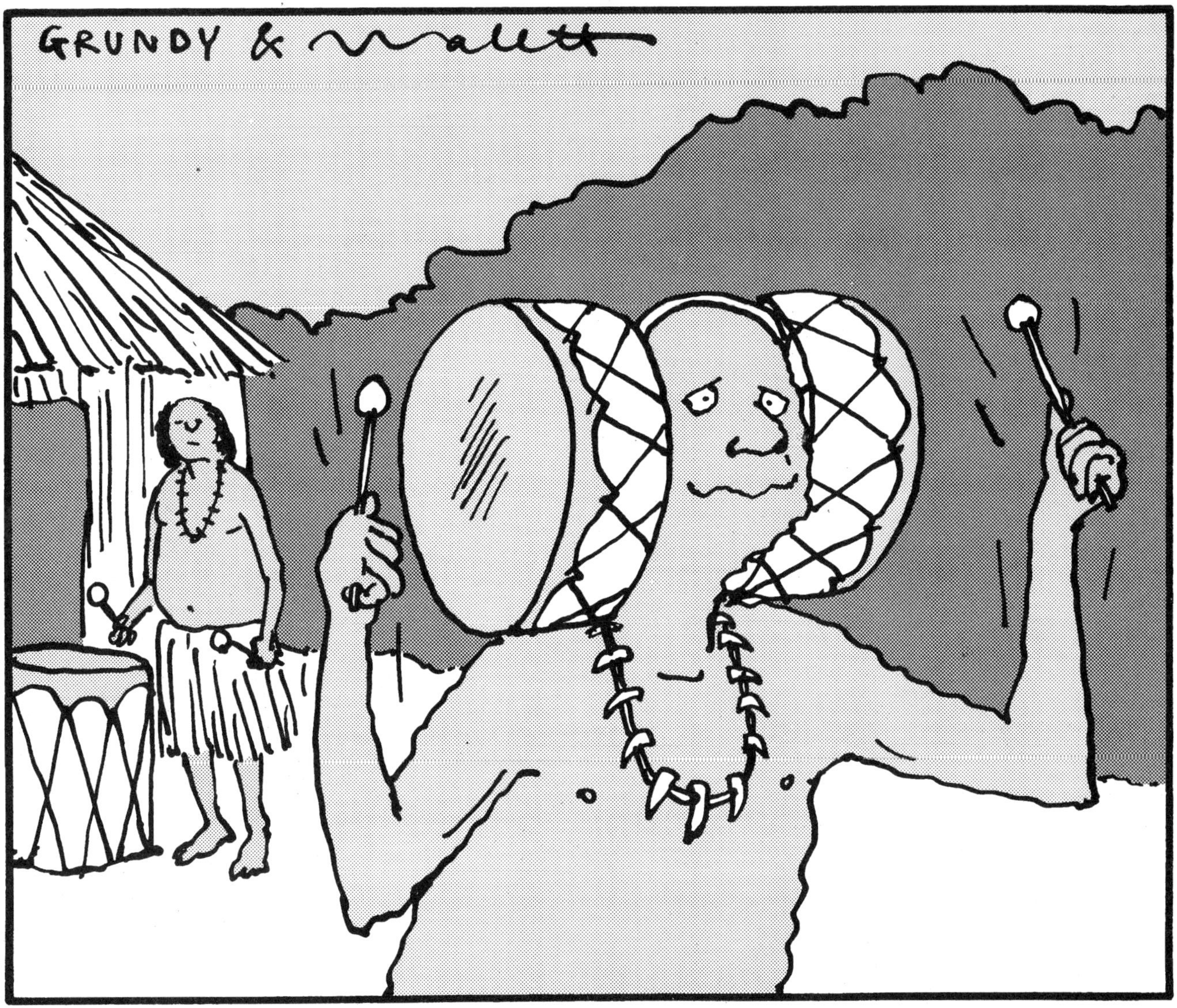
GRUNDY & Mallett

The first personal stereo.

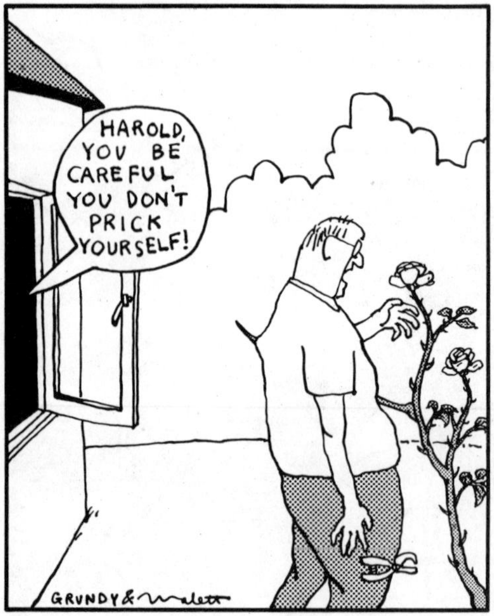
HAROLD, YOU BE CAREFUL YOU DON'T PRICK YOURSELF!

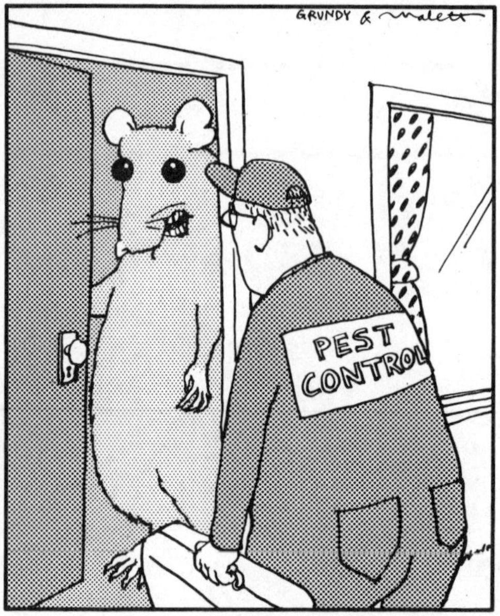
PEST CONTROL

"I'm sorry, no one is home at the moment."

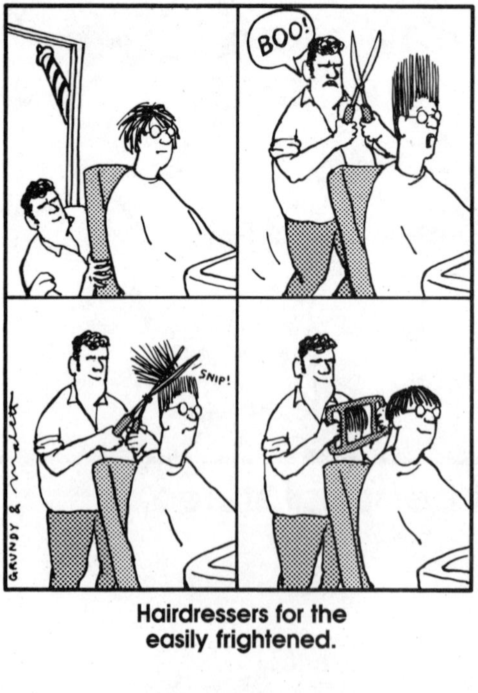
BOO!
SNIP!

Hairdressers for the easily frightened.

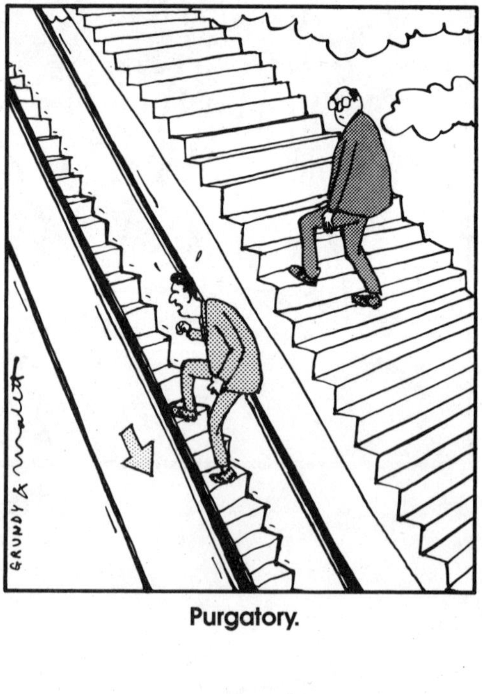

Purgatory.

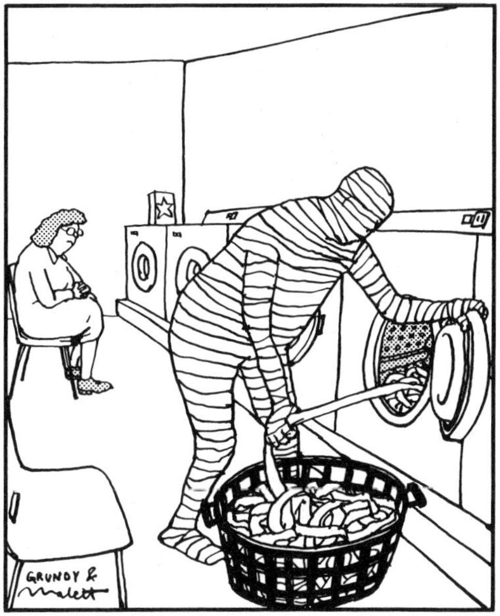
GRUNDY &
Malett

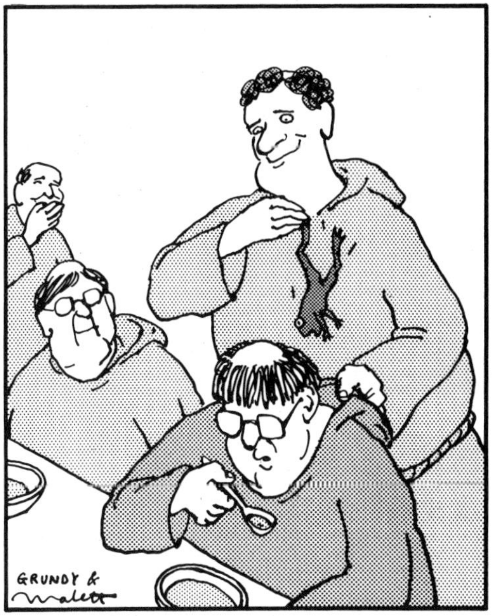
GRUNDY &
Malett

Brother Peter's vow of silence is about to end abruptly.

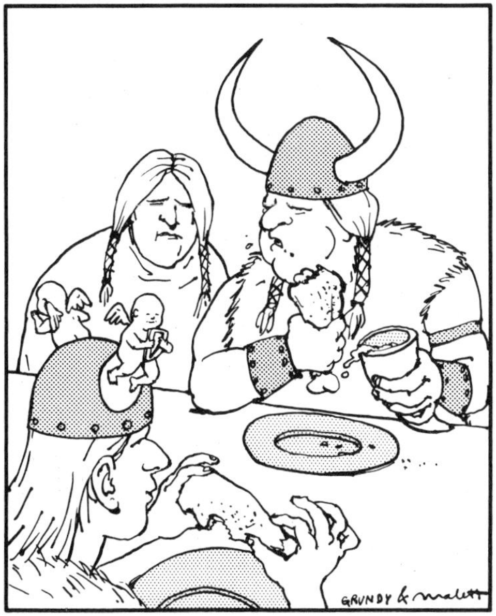
GRUNDY & Malett

"I worry about that boy."

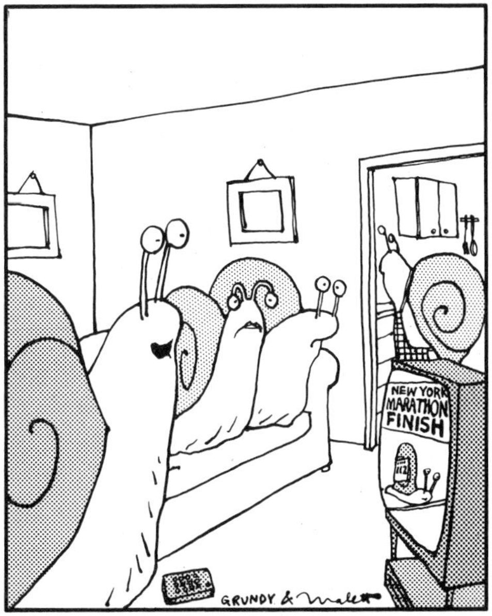
NEW YORK
MARATHON
FINISH
GRUNDY & Malett

"Finally, there's me crossing the line. Hilda videotaped me all the way. Hey! Let's play the whole thing back in slow motion!"

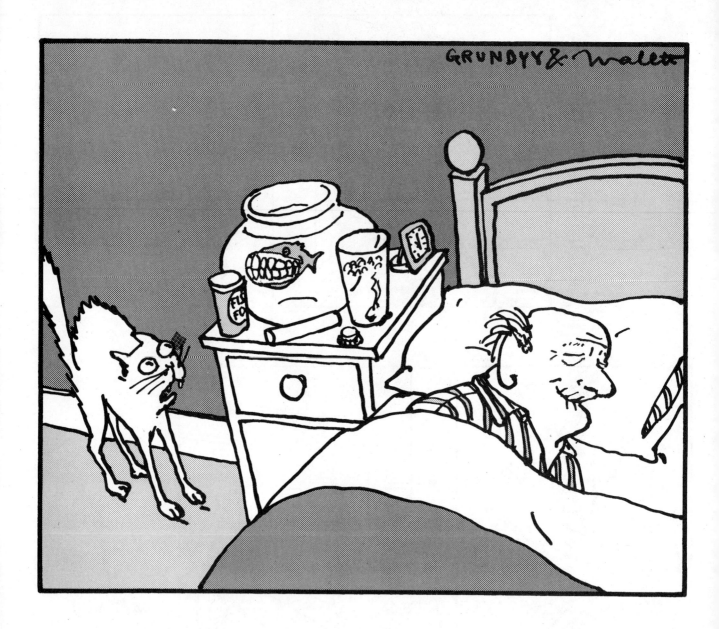

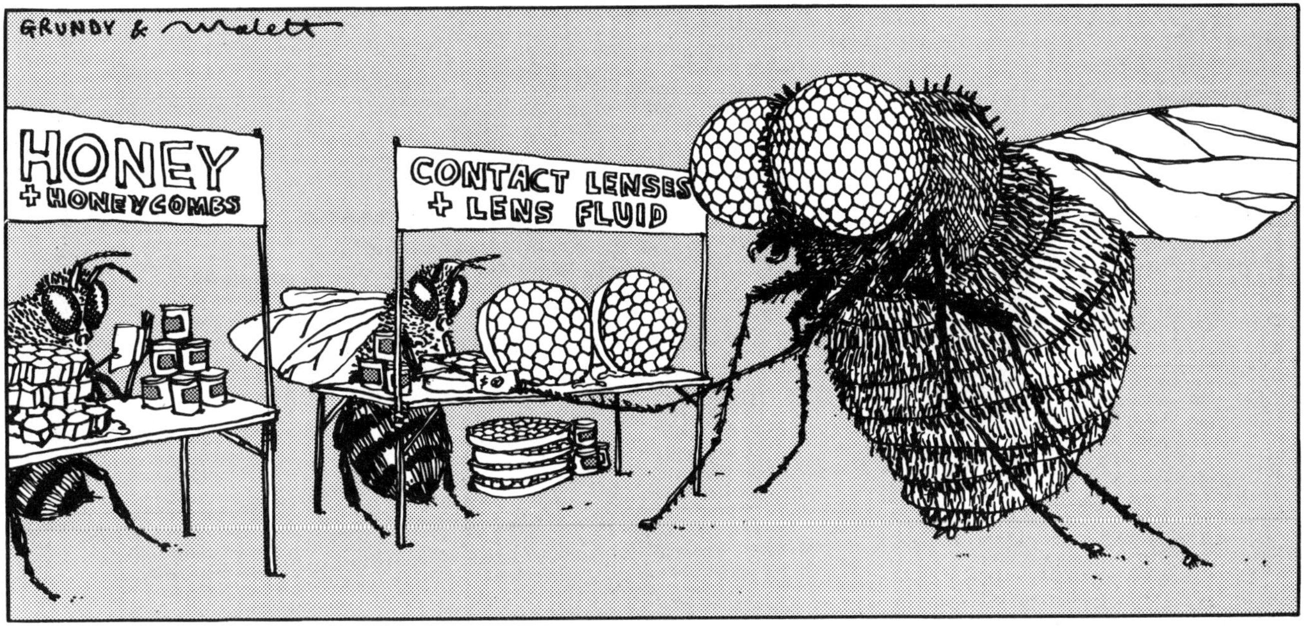
GRUNDY & Malett
HONEY
+ HONEYCOMBS
CONTACT LENSES
+ LENS FLUID

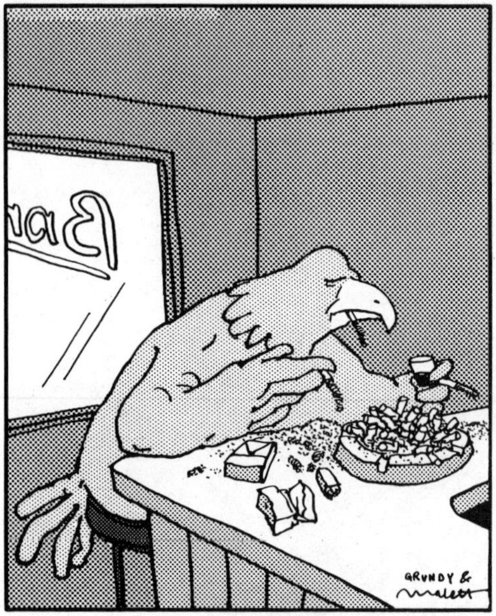

The phoenix that didn't rise from the ashes.

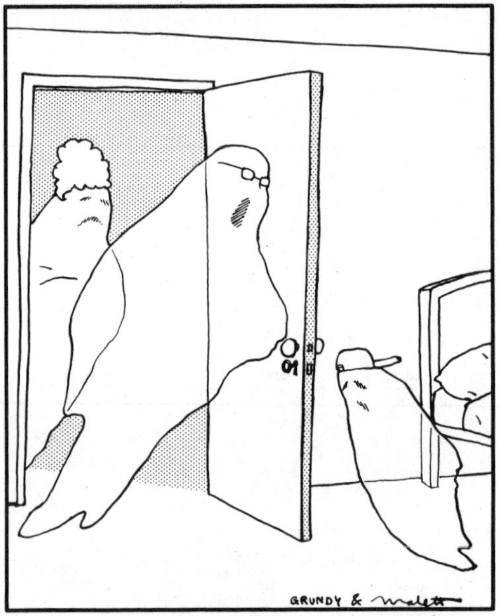

"You're grounded! And don't let me catch you walking through the walls!"

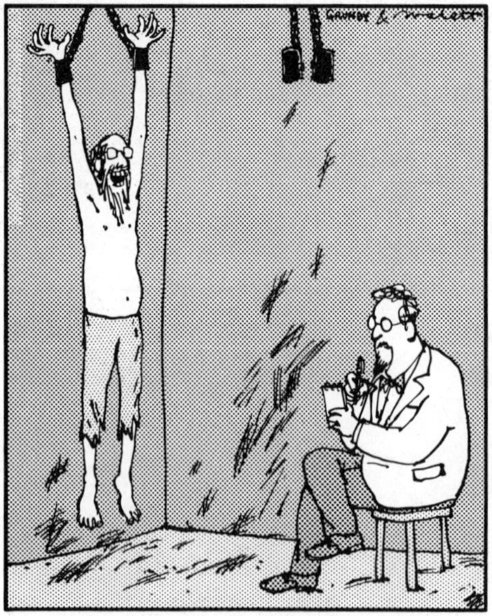

"Call me weird, but I feel good!"

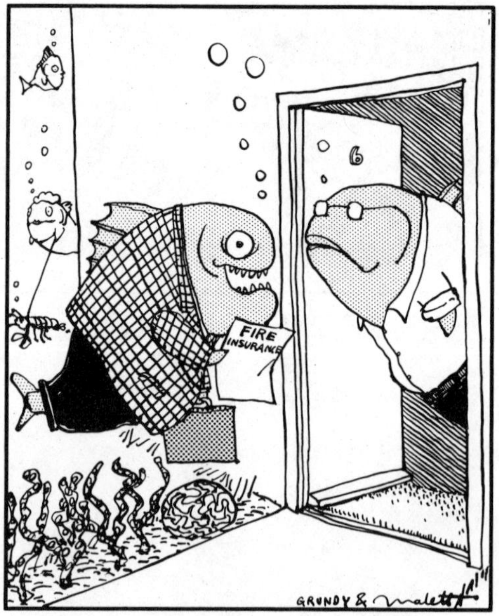
FIRE INSURANCE

"Can I interest you in an exciting new policy?"

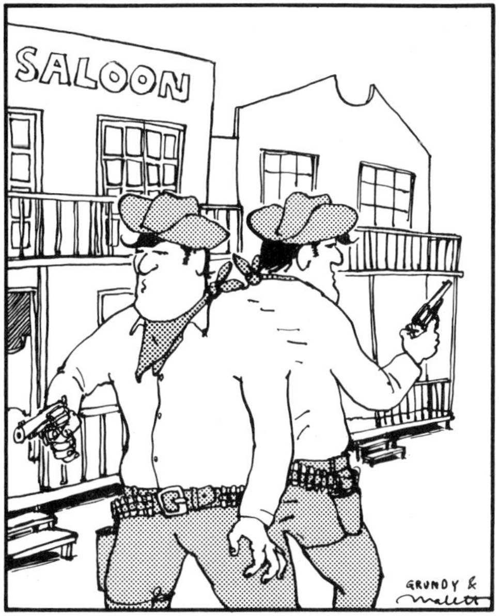
SALOON

Siamese twins Jed and Tony never had to say, "Watch my back!"

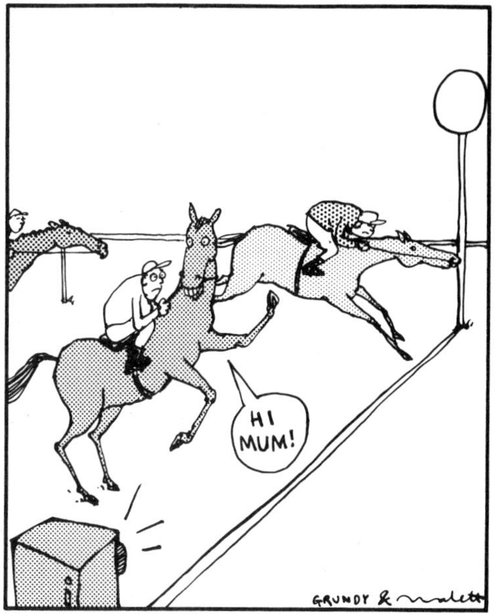
HI MUM!

Photo finish.

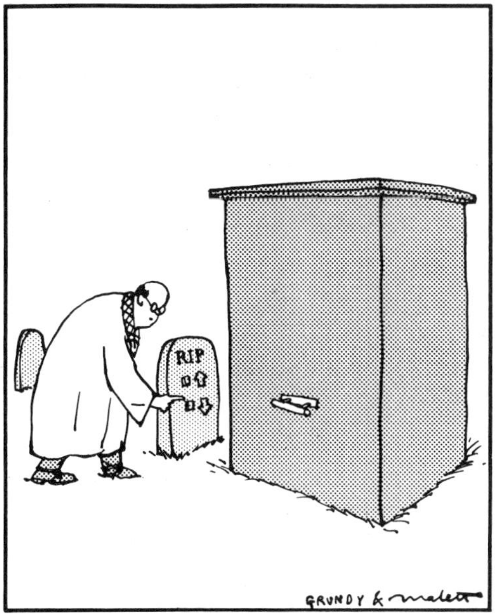
RIP

Elevator graveyard.

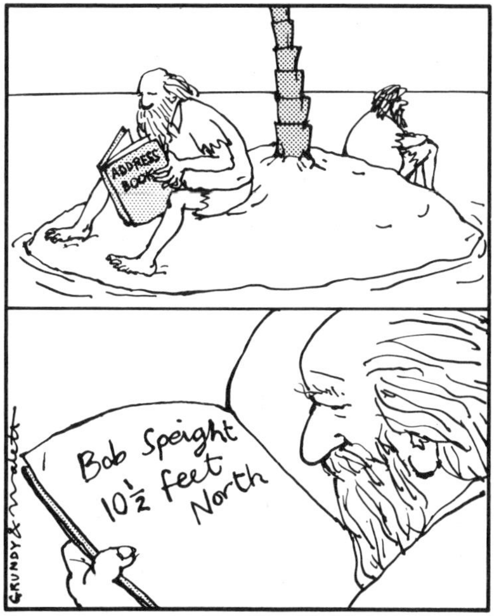
ADDRESS BOOK
Bob Speight
10½ feet North

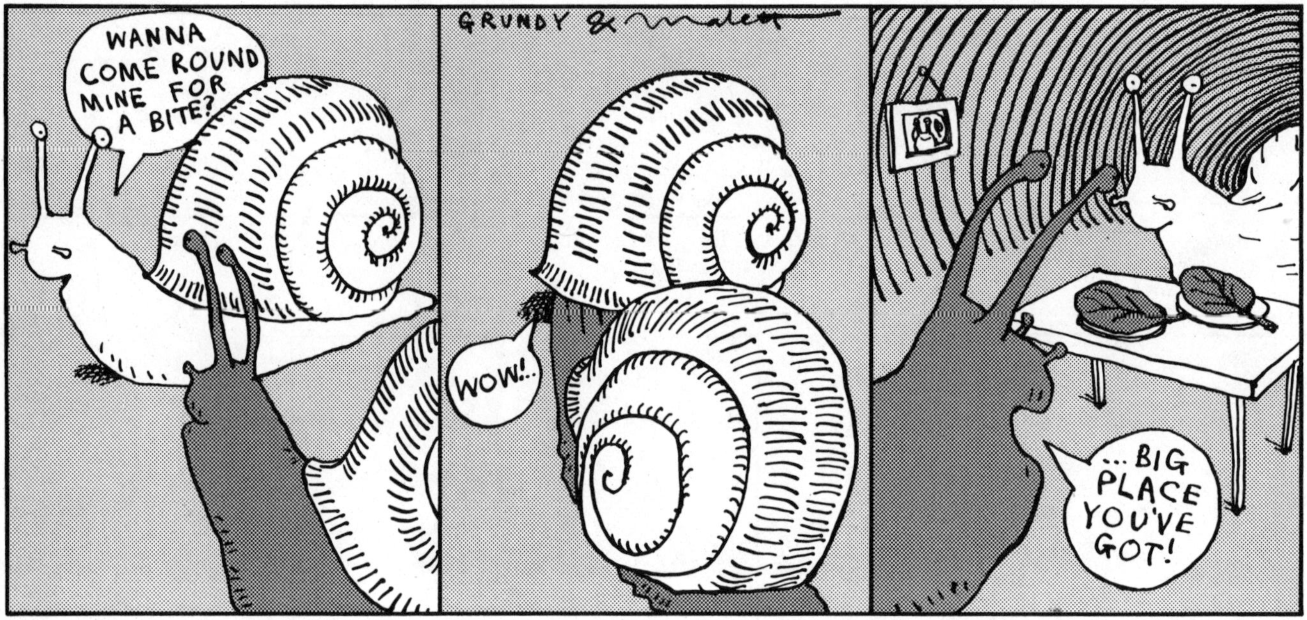
WANNA COME ROUND MINE FOR A BITE?
GRUNDY &
WOW!..
...BIG PLACE YOU'VE GOT!

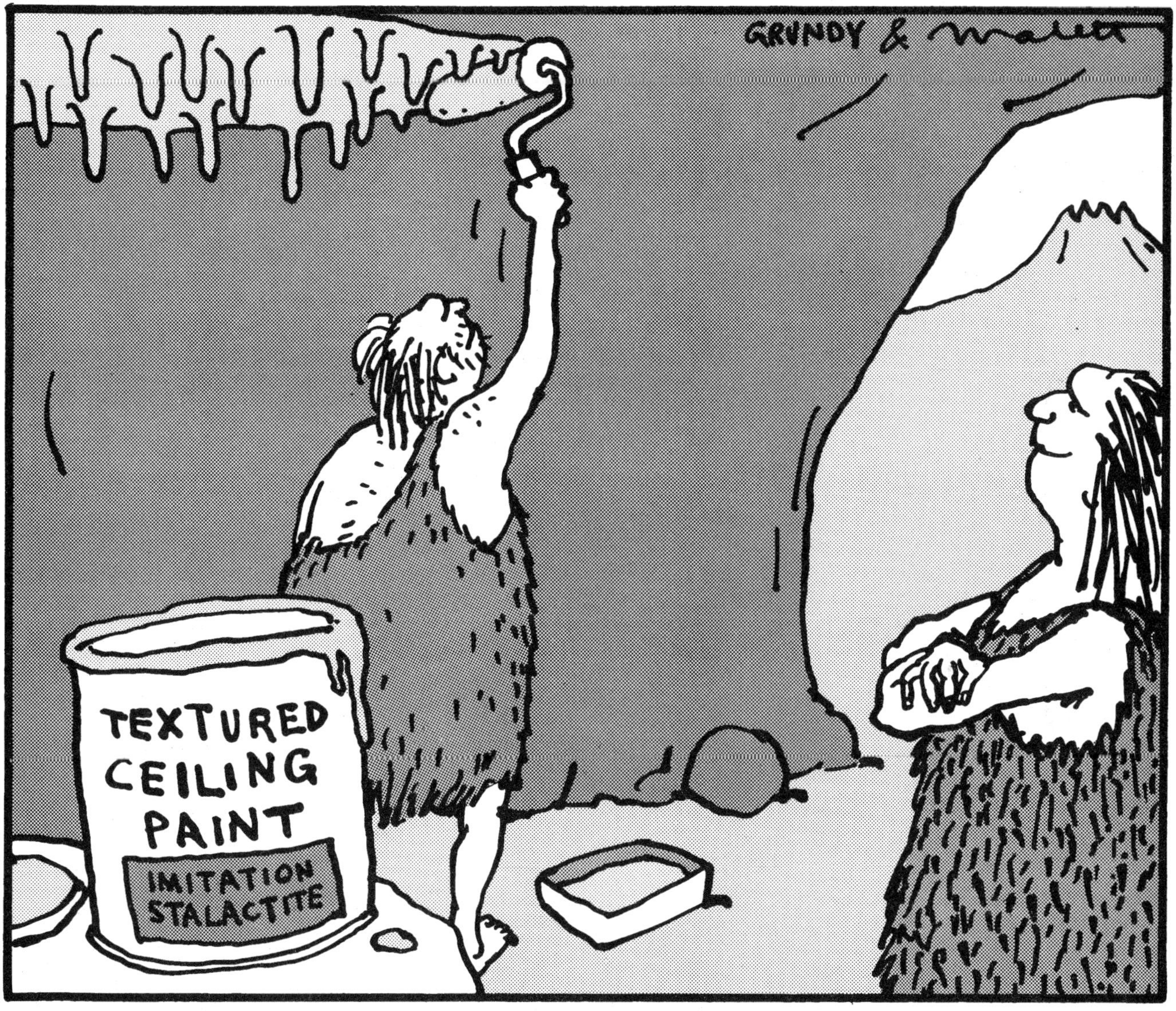
GRUNDY & malett
TEXTURED
CEILING
PAINT
IMITATION
STALACTITE

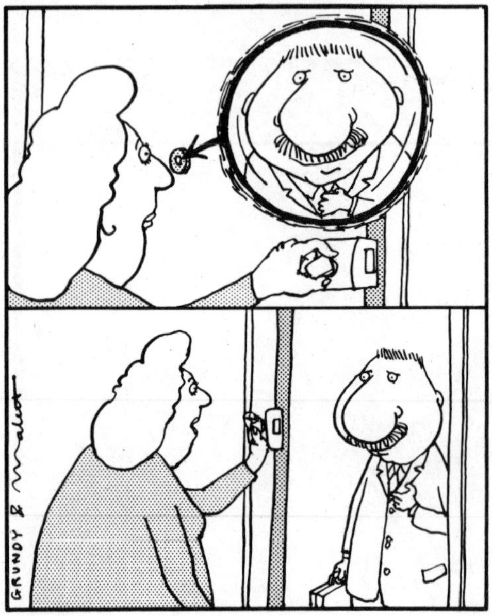
GRUNDY & MALETT

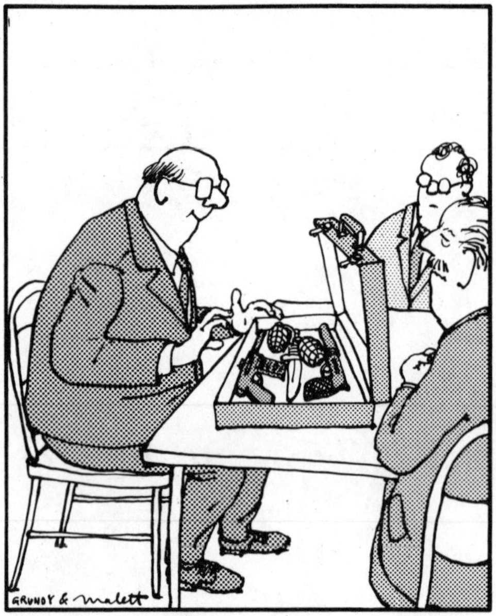
GRUNDY & MALETT

Julian starts a hostile takeover bid.

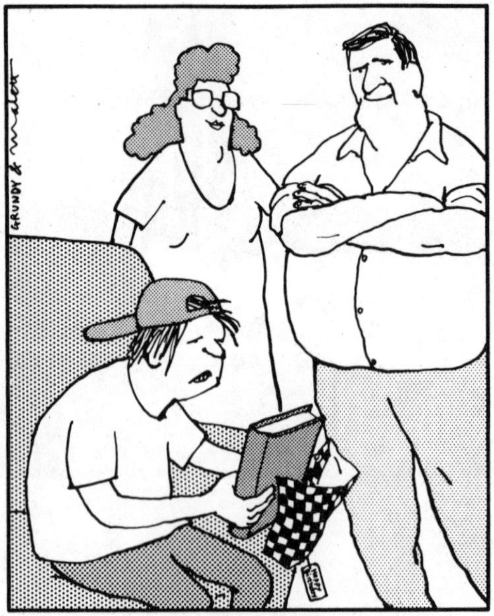
GRUNDY & MALETT

"Oh, a book! But I've already got one."

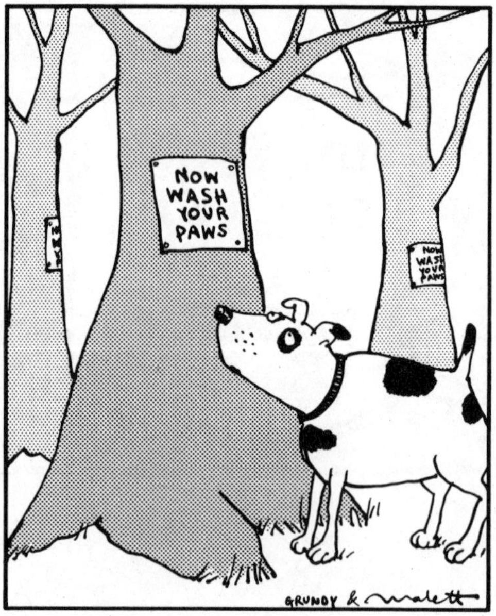
NOW WASH YOUR PAWS
NOW WASH YOUR PAWS
GRUNDY & MALETT

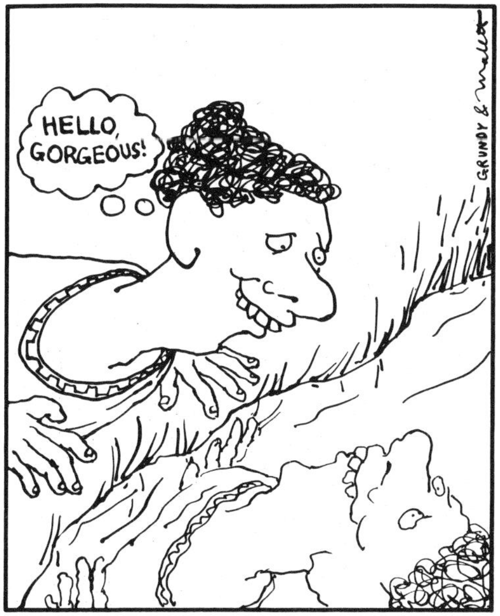
HELLO, GORGEOUS!
GRUNDY & Malett

Narcissus not only was conceited, but also had appalling taste.

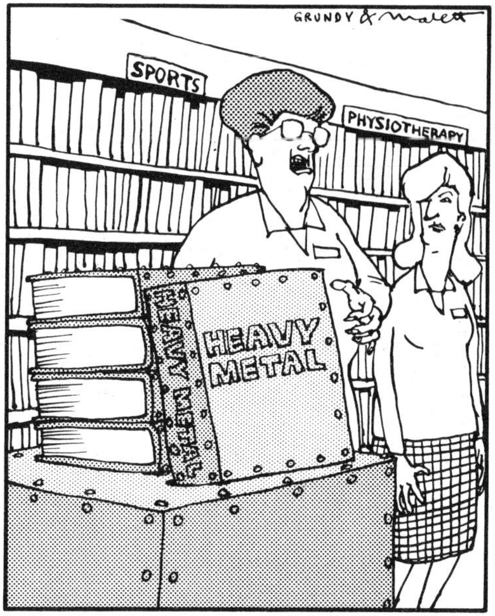
GRUNDY & Malett
SPORTS
PHYSIOTHERAPY
HEAVY METAL
HEAVY METAL

"Great book! Once you put it down, you can't pick it up."

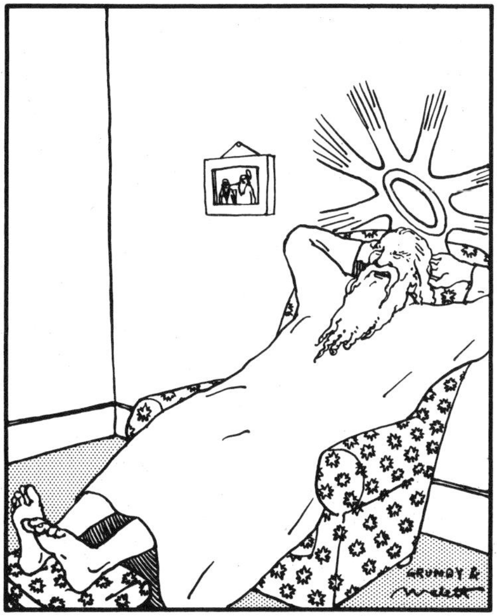
GRUNDY & Malett

"Thank me it's Friday!"

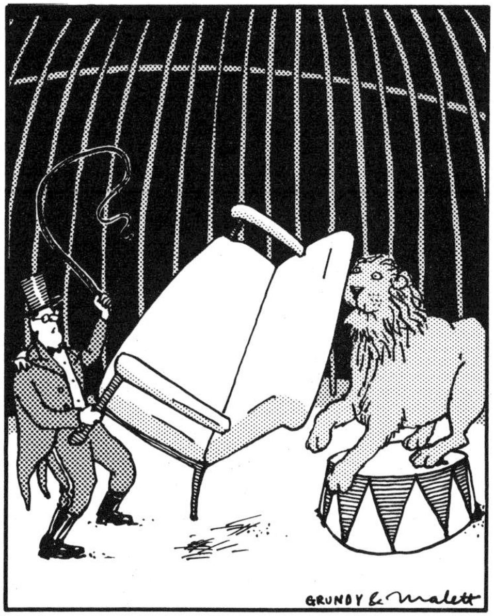
GRUNDY & Malett

The lion tamer who takes no chances.

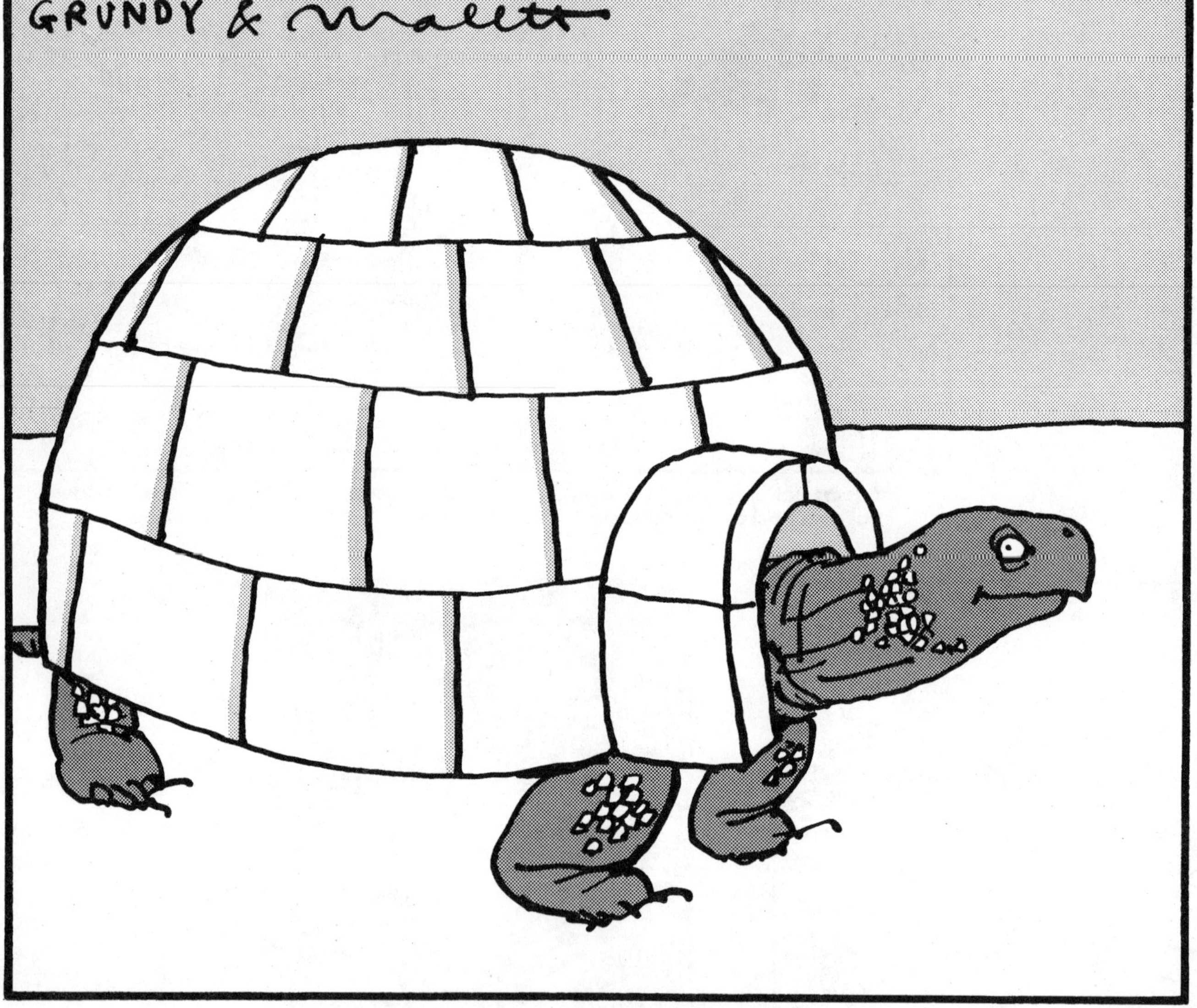
GRUNDY & Mallett

Tortoise of the North.

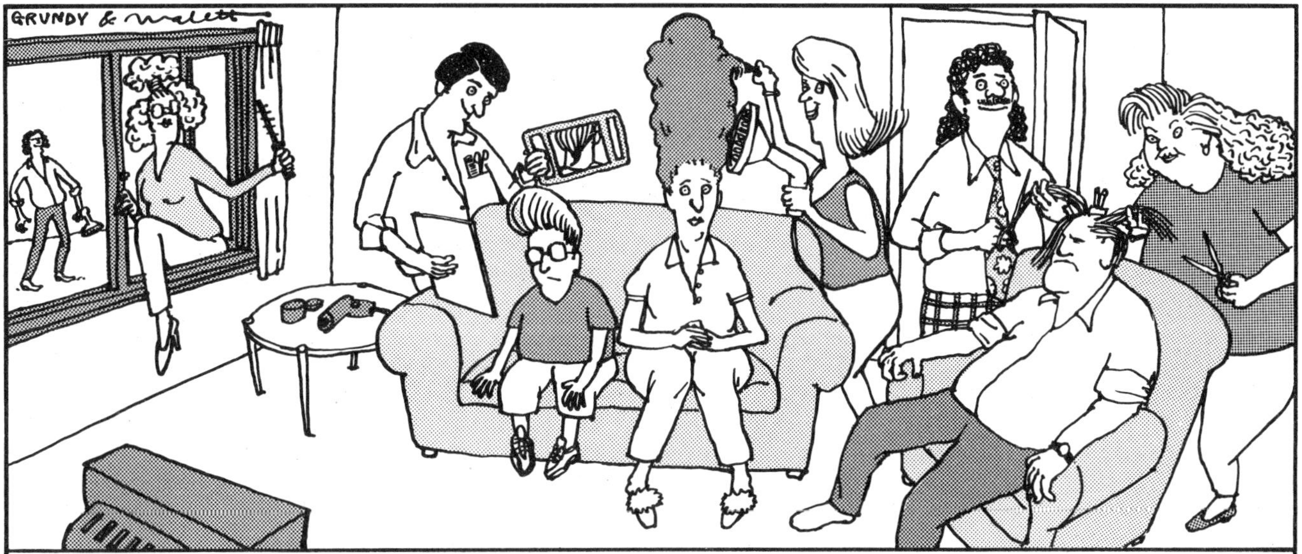
GRUNDY & Malett

Attack of the Hairdo People.

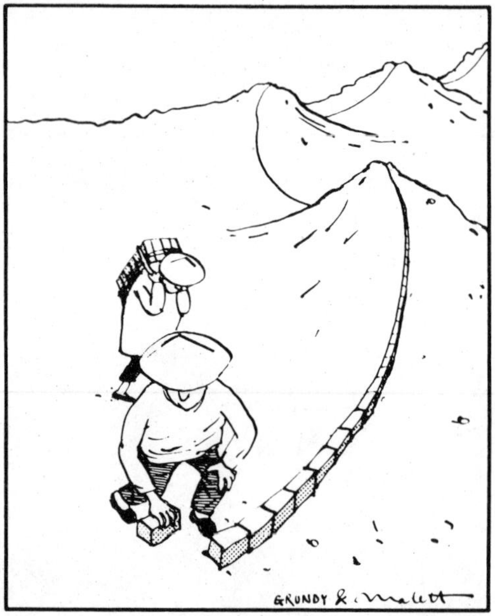
GRUNDY & Malett

The Not-So-Great Wall of China.

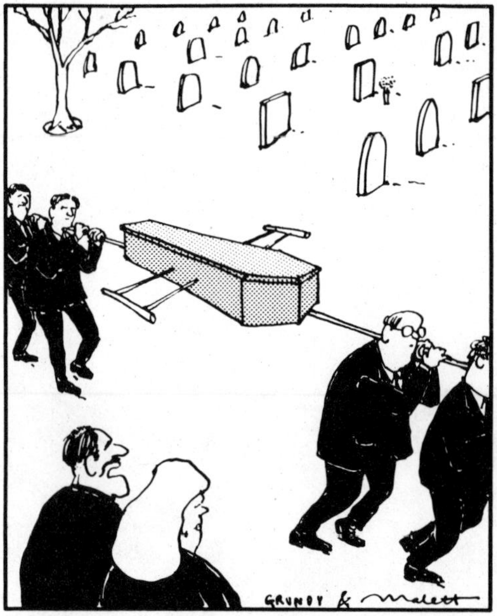
GRUNDY & Malett

"He was the best tightrope walker in the business."

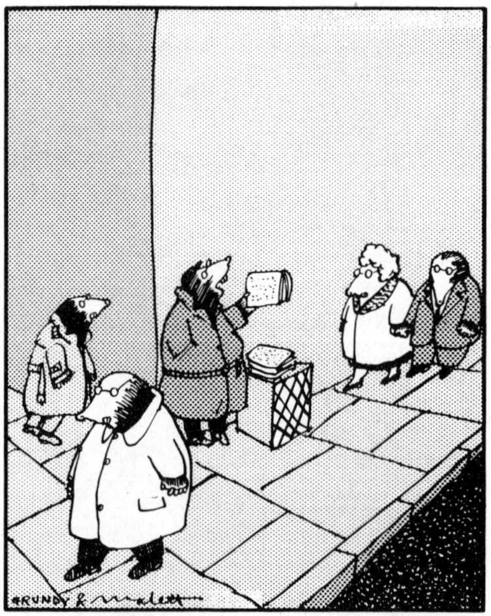
GRUNDY & Malett

"Feel all about it, feel all about it!"

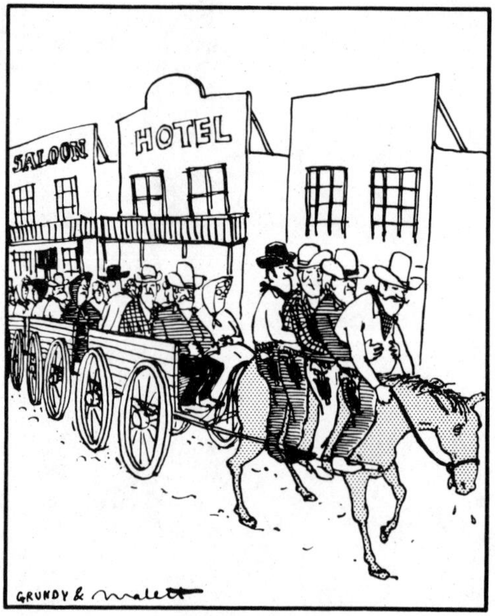
SALOON
HOTEL
GRUNDY & Malett

One-horse town.

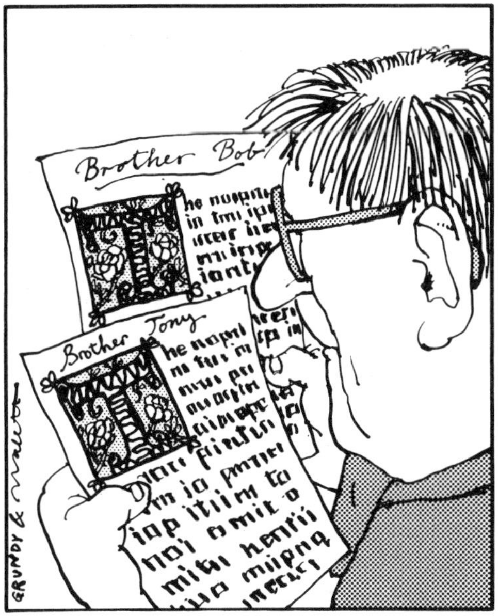
Brother Bob
Brother Tony
GRUNDY & Malett

Father Dominic suspects cheating on the theology exam.

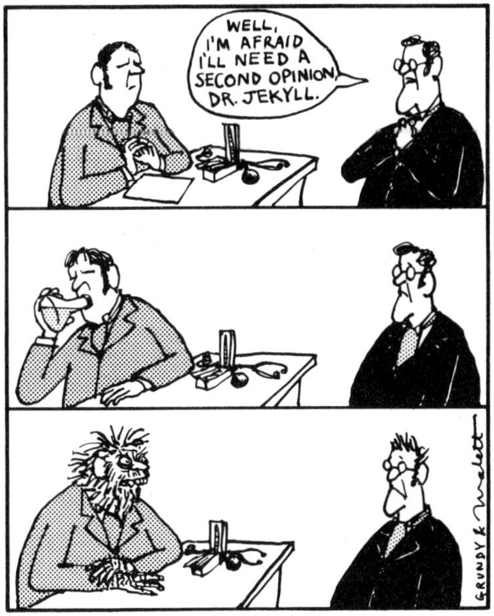
WELL, I'M AFRAID I'LL NEED A SECOND OPINION, DR. JEKYLL.
GRUNDY & Malett

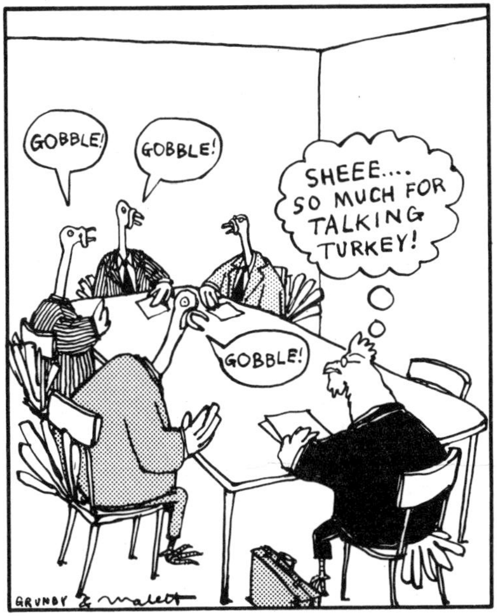
GOBBLE!
GOBBLE!
SHEEE.... SO MUCH FOR TALKING TURKEY!
GOBBLE!
GRUNDY & Malett

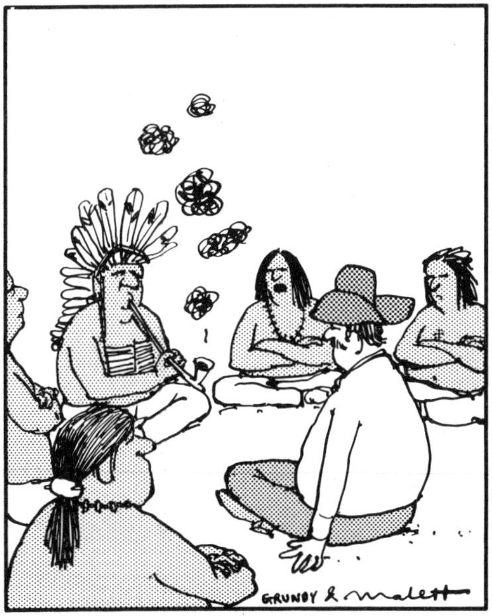
GRUNDY & Malett

"Chief says . . . surgeon general warns that smoking damages health."

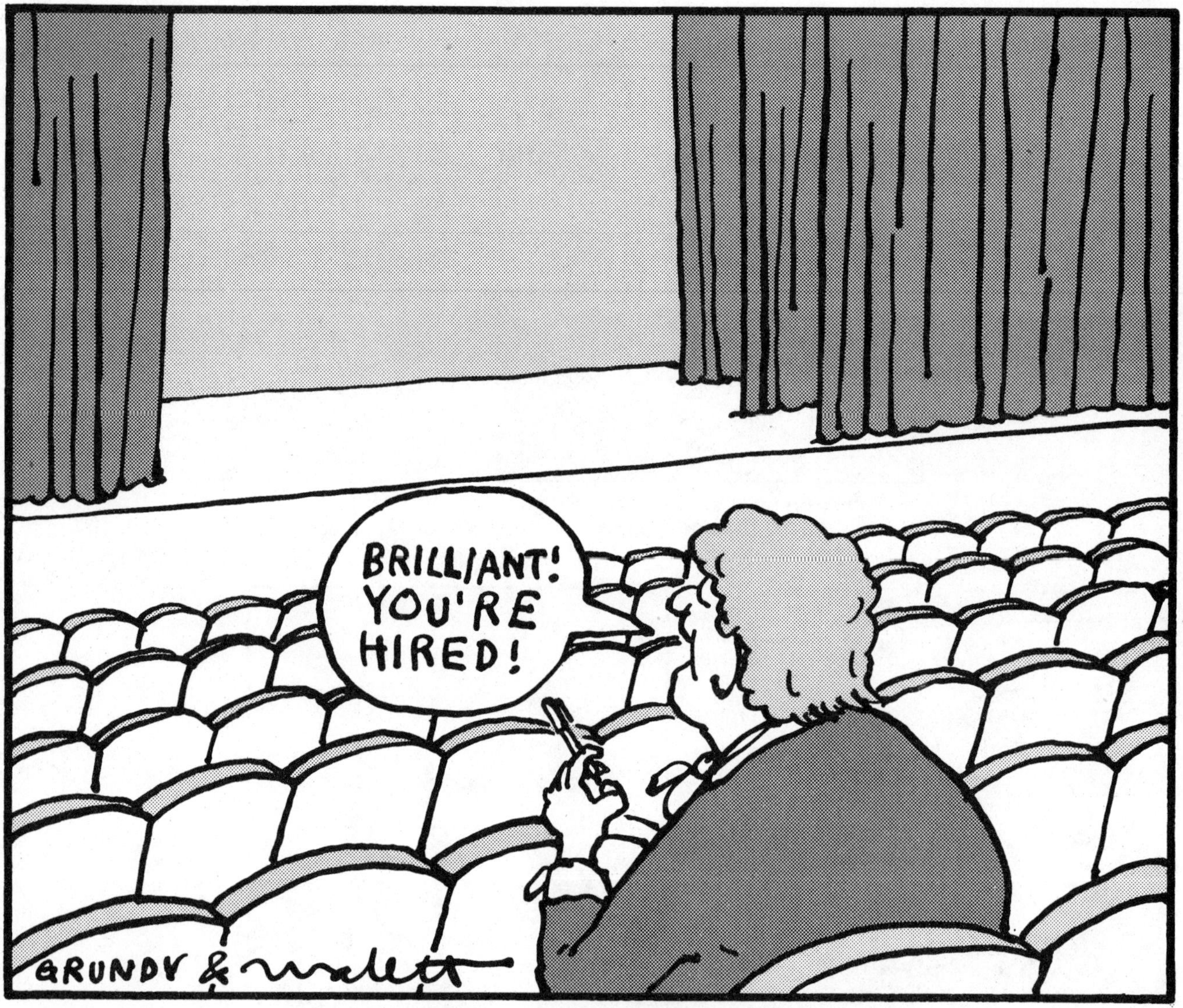
BRILLIANT! YOU'RE HIRED!
GRUNDY & MALLETT

At an audition for the lead role in
"The Invisible Man."

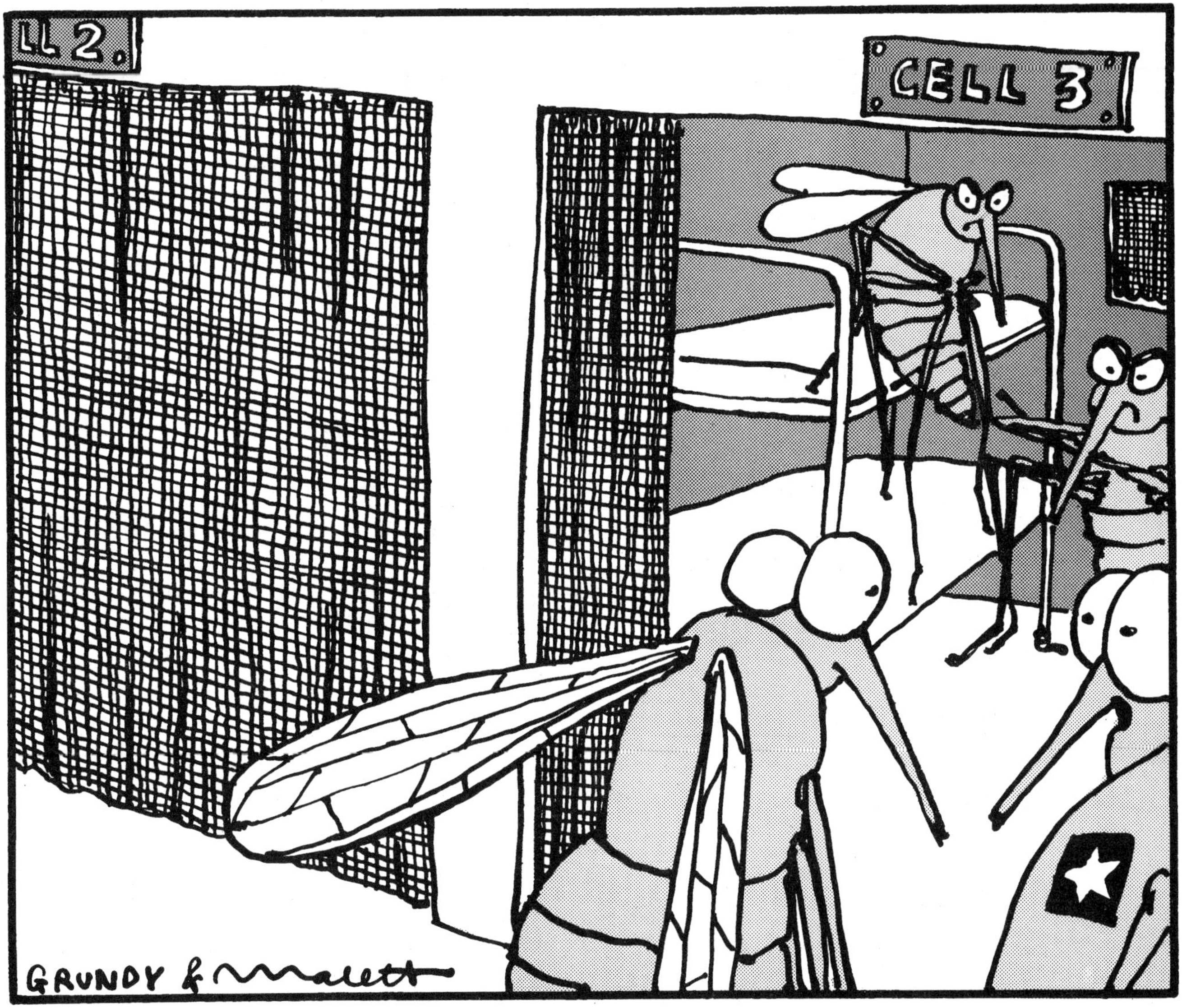
LL 2.
CELL 3
GRUNDY & Malett

"Make sure you pull that net across properly. Any little gap and they'll find it."

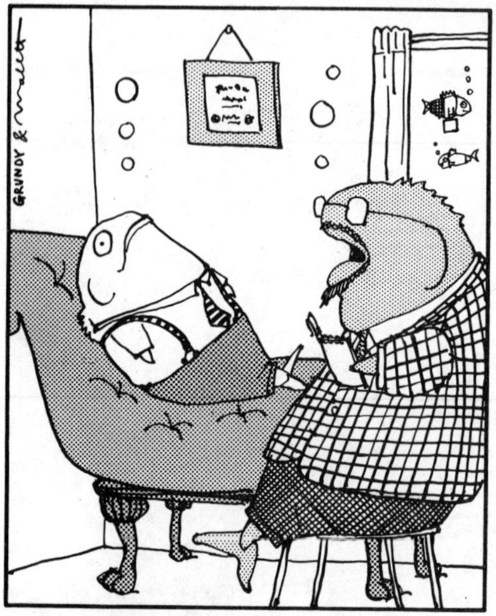
GRUNDY & Malett

"And how long have you imagined you can smell smoke?"

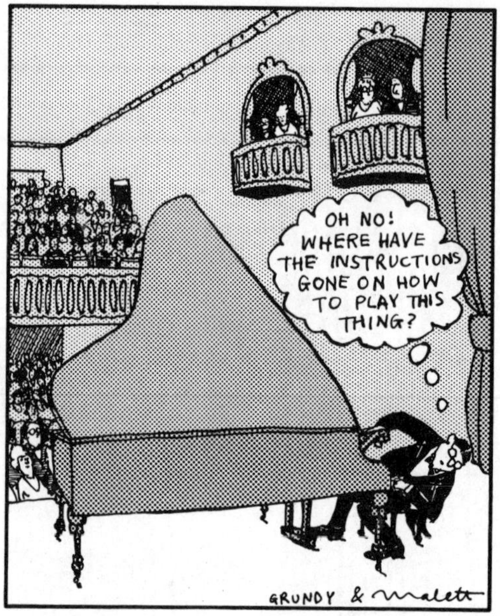
OH NO! WHERE HAVE THE INSTRUCTIONS GONE ON HOW TO PLAY THIS THING?
GRUNDY & Malett

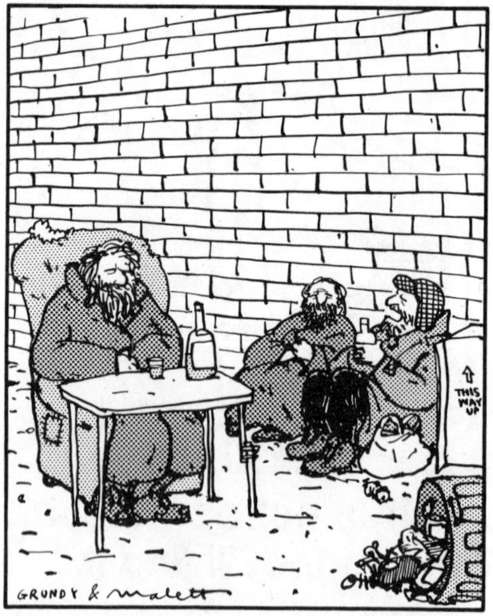
THIS WAY UP
GRUNDY & Malett

"Typical! Red wins 10 bucks in the lottery and says it won't change his life."

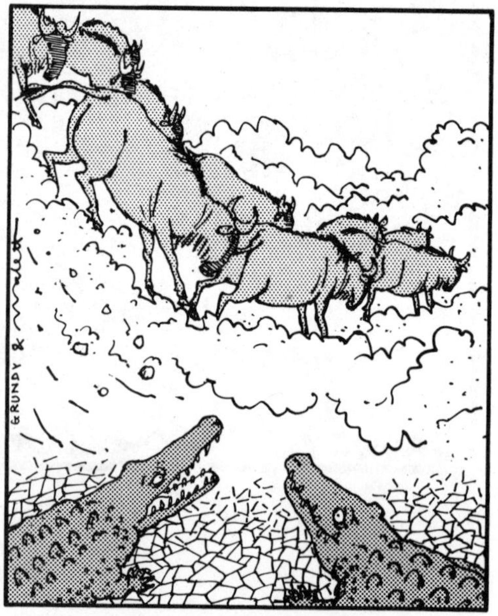
GRUNDY & Malett

"Wonderful! That time of year again, and the river dries up!"

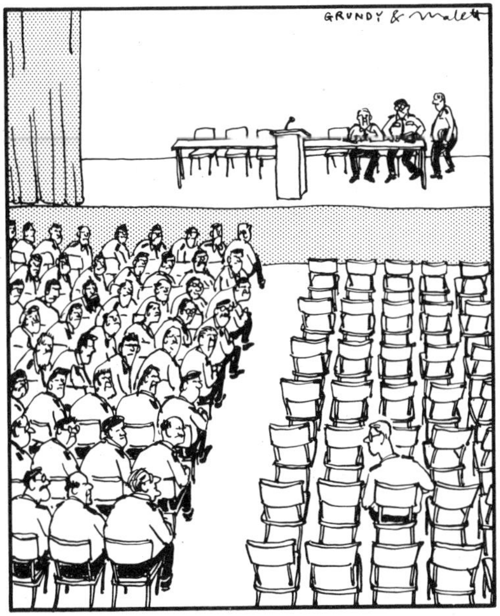

Harold has the awful feeling that the annual meeting for co-pilots could be tomorrow.

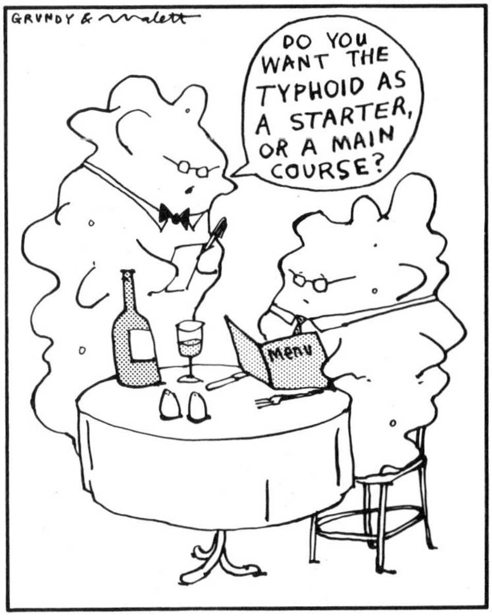
DO YOU WANT THE TYPHOID AS A STARTER, OR A MAIN COURSE?
Menu

Restaurant for white blood cells.

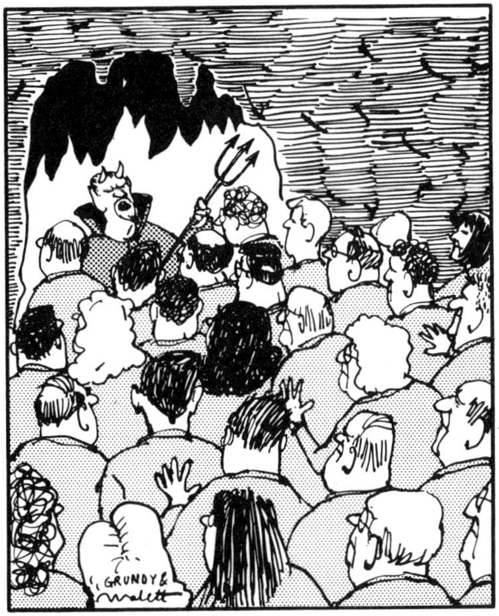

"OK, OK, quit shoving at the back."

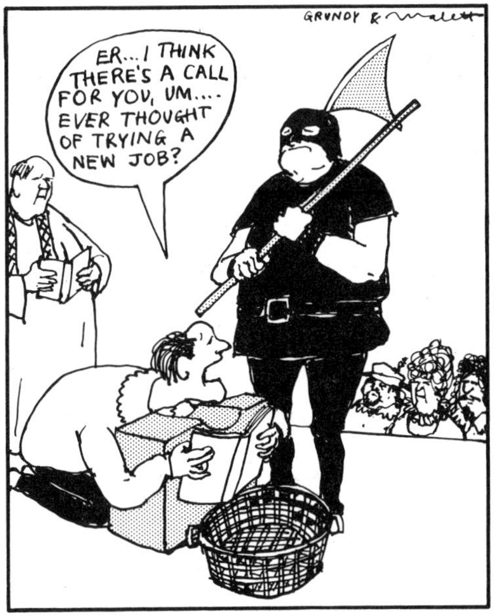
ER... I THINK THERE'S A CALL FOR YOU, UM.... EVER THOUGHT OF TRYING A NEW JOB?

John tries every trick in the book.

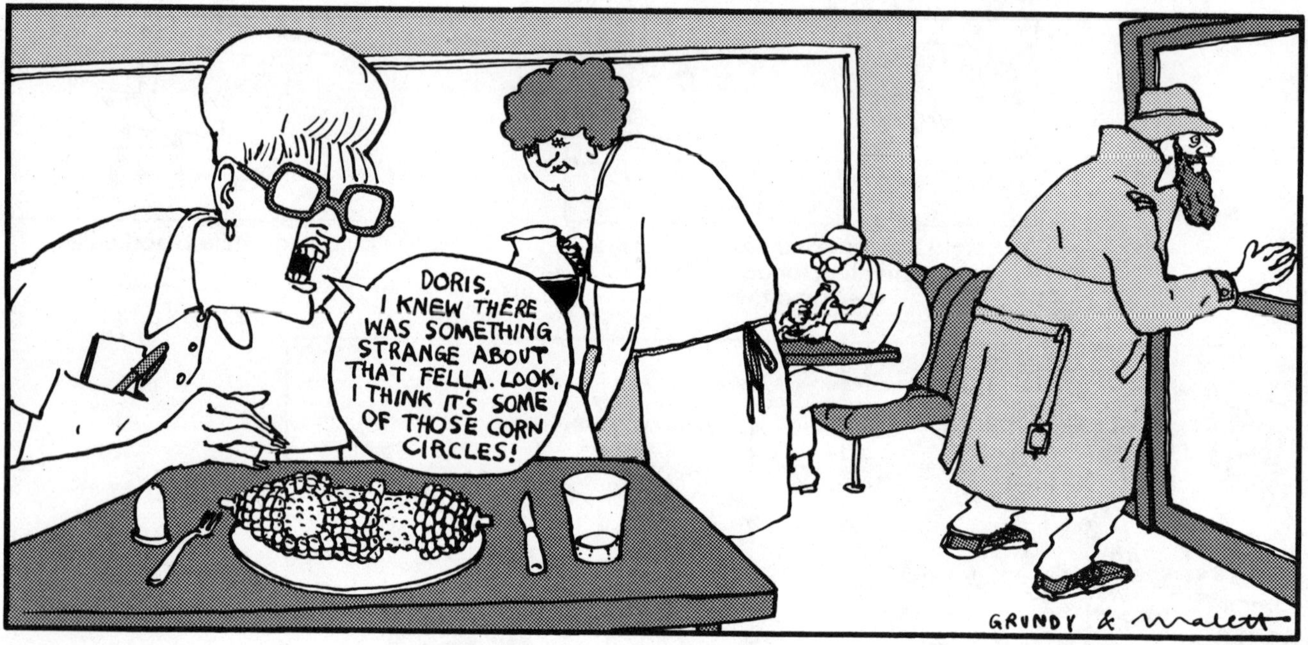
DORIS, I KNEW THERE WAS SOMETHING STRANGE ABOUT THAT FELLA. LOOK, I THINK IT'S SOME OF THOSE CORN CIRCLES!
GRUNDY & MALETT

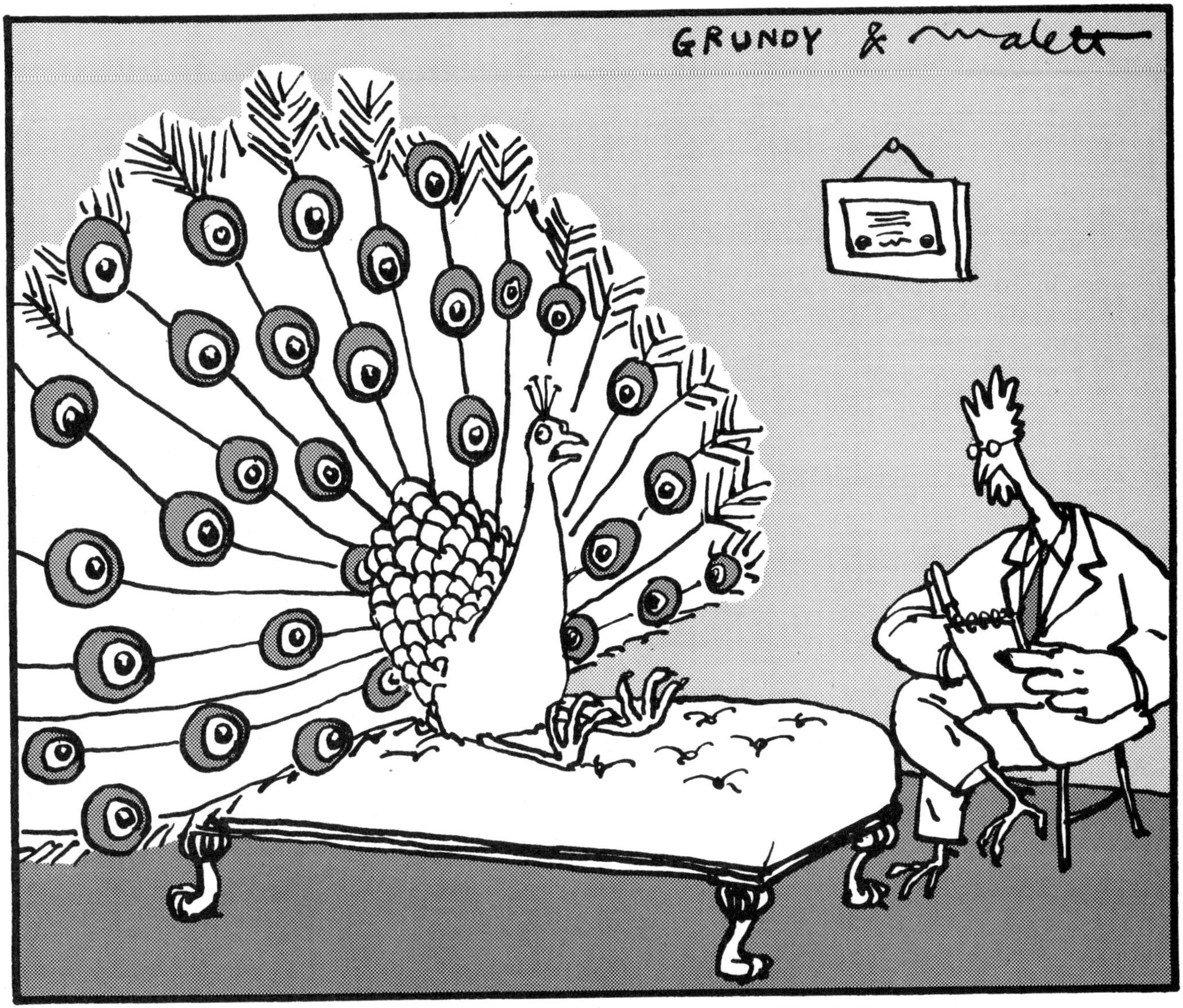
GRUNDY & malett

"I keep having this feeling that I'm being watched."

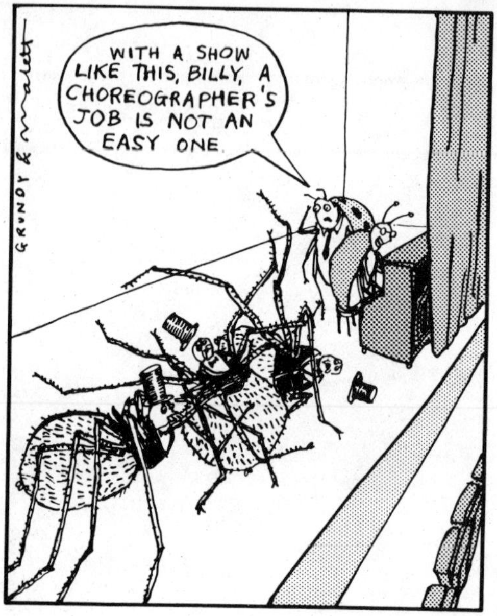
WITH A SHOW LIKE THIS, BILLY, A CHOREOGRAPHER'S JOB IS NOT AN EASY ONE.
GRUNDY & Malett

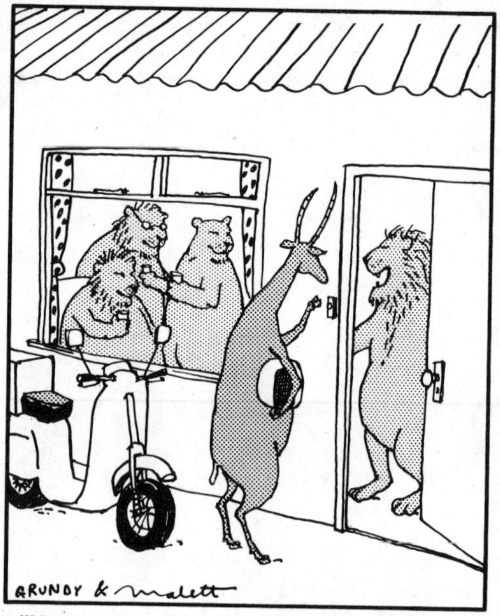
GRUNDY & Malett
"Hey, anyone here order an antelope?"

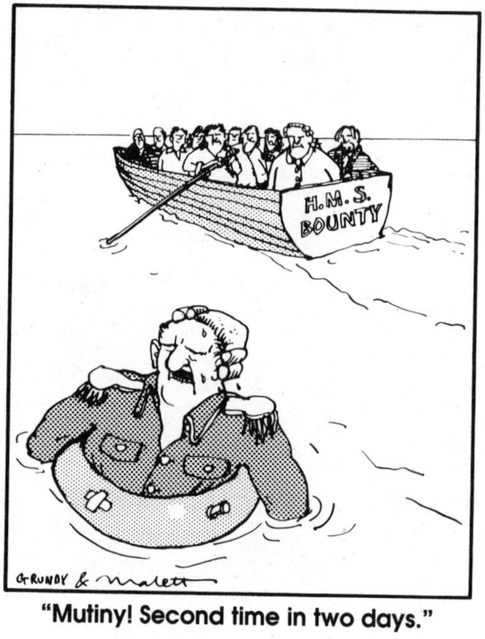
H.M.S. BOUNTY
GRUNDY & Malett
"Mutiny! Second time in two days."

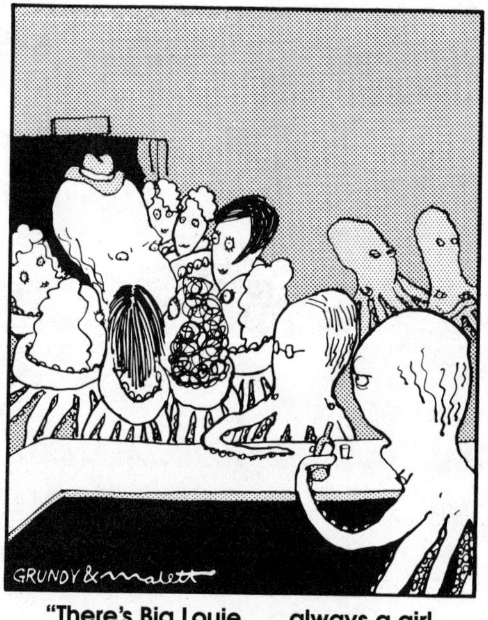
GRUNDY & Malett
"There's Big Louie . . . always a girl on every arm."

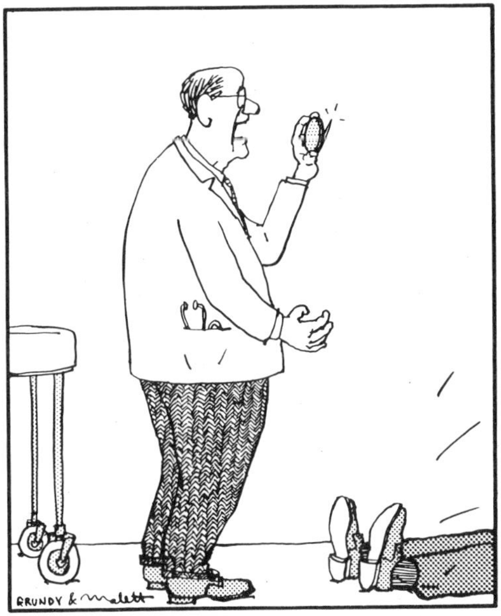
GRUNDY & Malett

"In recognition of your courage in overcoming the fear of injections . . ."

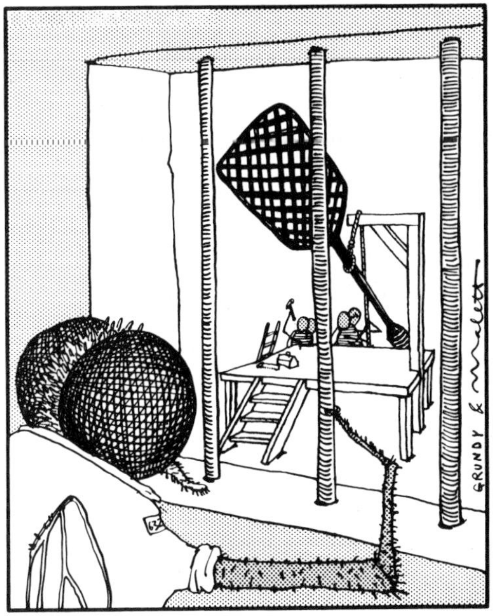
GRUNDY & Malett

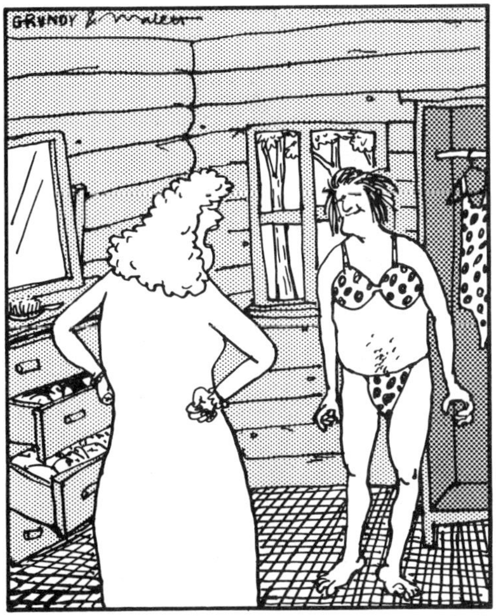
GRUNDY & Malett

"No, no! ME Jane, YOU Tarzan!"

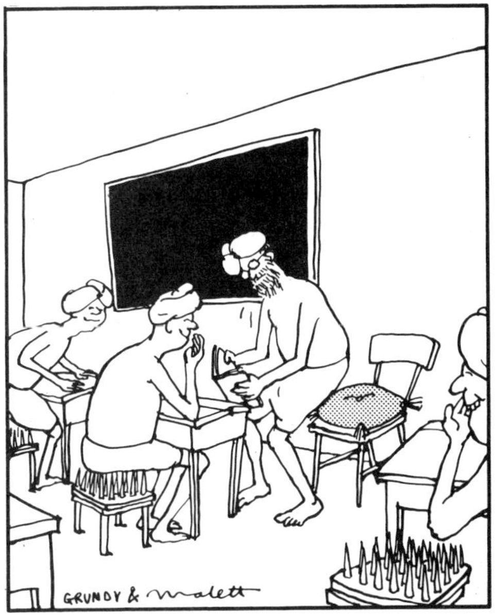
GRUNDY & Malett

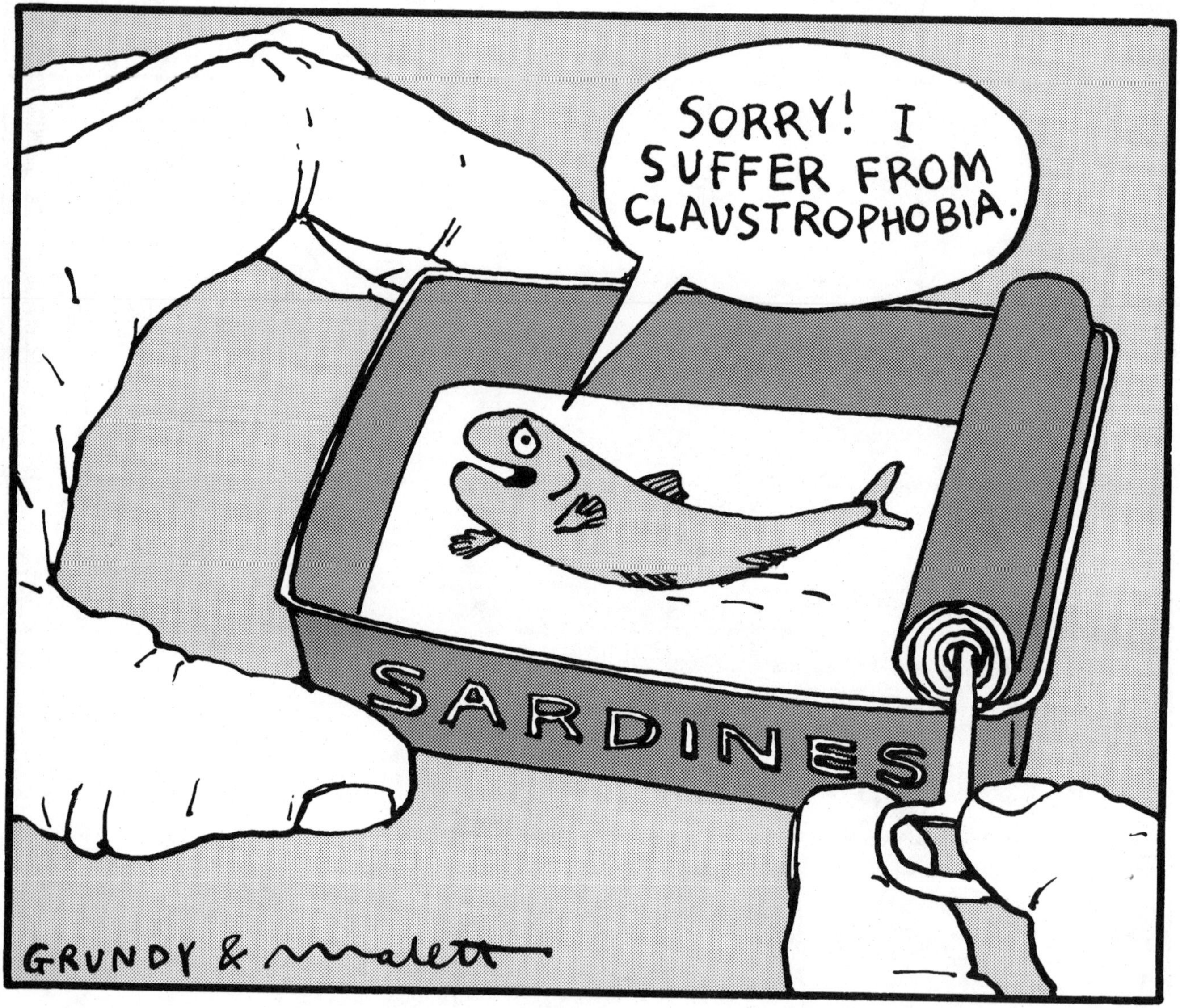
SORRY! I SUFFER FROM CLAUSTROPHOBIA.
SARDINES
GRUNDY & Malett

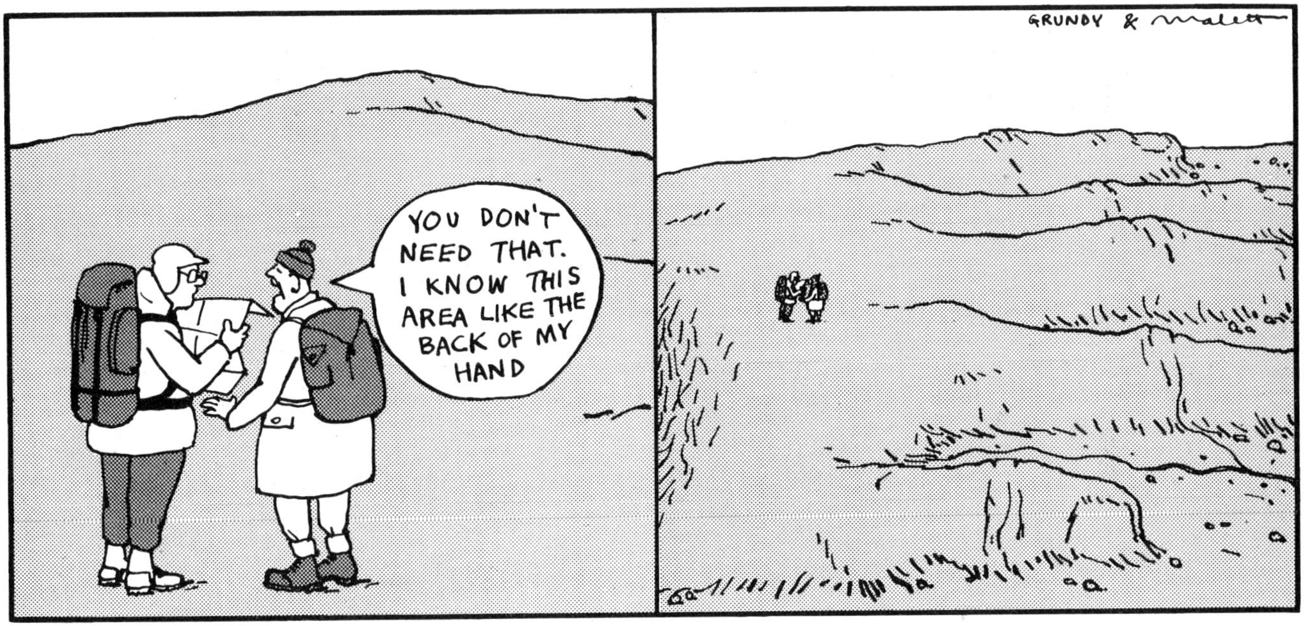
YOU DON'T NEED THAT. I KNOW THIS AREA LIKE THE BACK OF MY HAND
GRUNDY & Malett

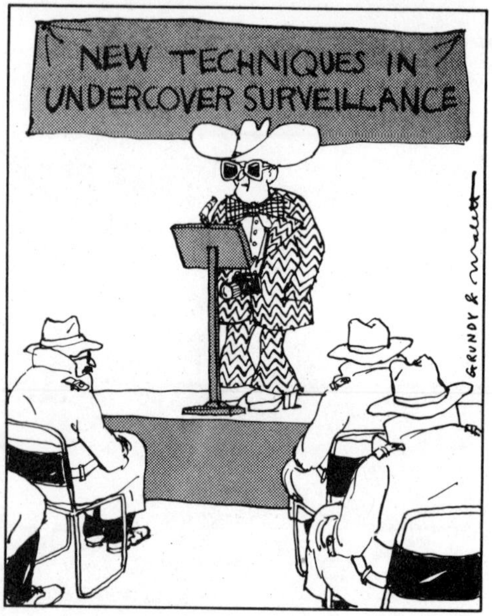
NEW TECHNIQUES IN UNDERCOVER SURVEILLANCE
GRUNDY & Malett

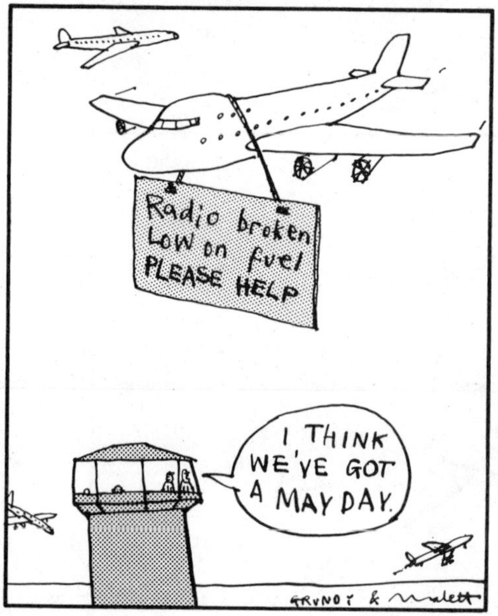
Radio broken
Low on fuel
PLEASE HELP
I THINK WE'VE GOT A MAYDAY.
GRUNDY & Malett

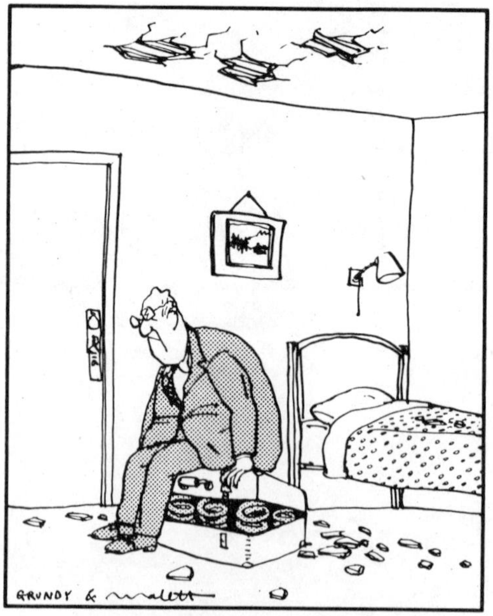
GRUNDY & Malett

High-tension-spring salesman.

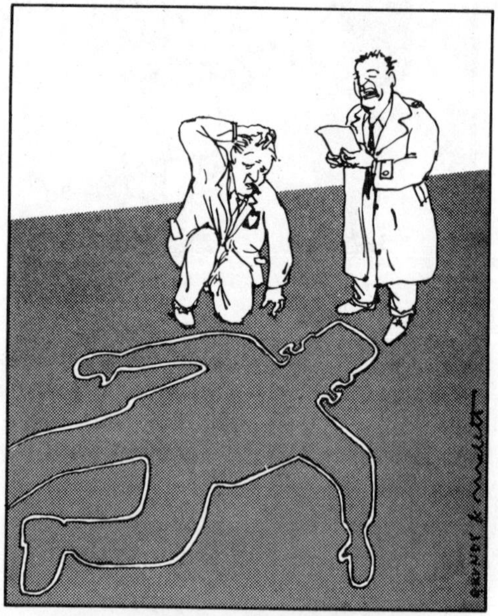
GRUNDY & Malett

"This is weird, Chief. The lab says the fingerprints and dental records don't belong to the same person. Who was this guy?"

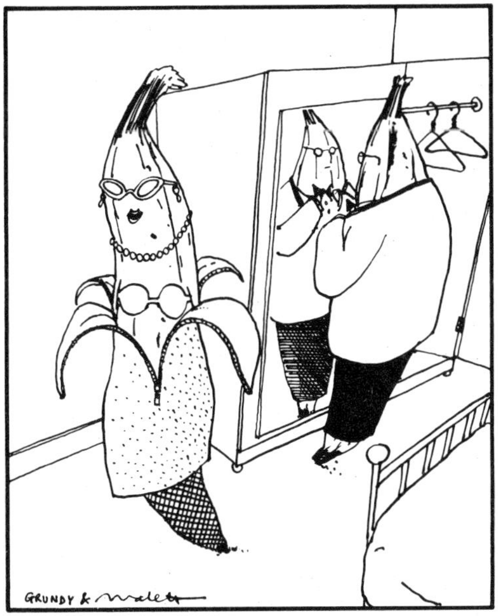
GRUNDY & Malett

"Zip me up, will you, darling?"

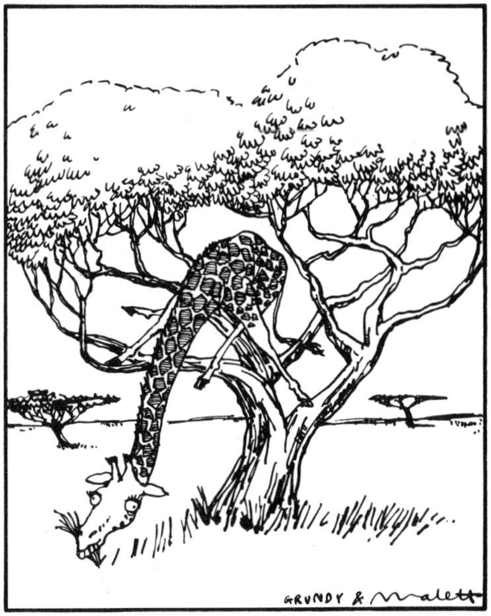
GRUNDY & Malett

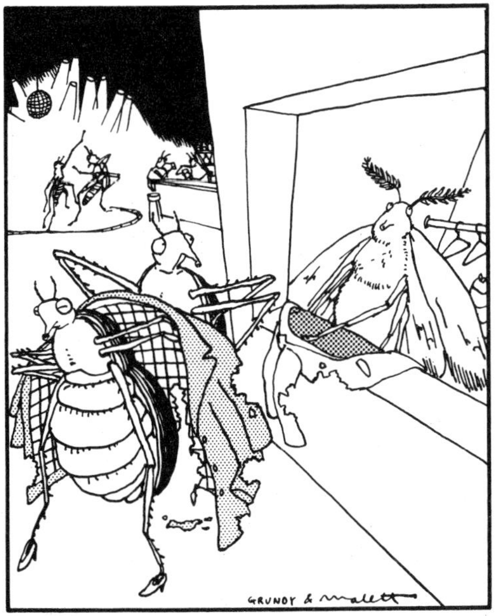
GRUNDY & Malett

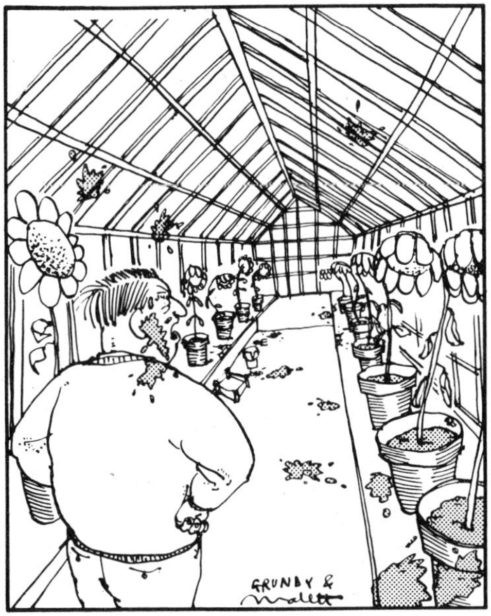
GRUNDY &
Malett

"OK, who started it?"

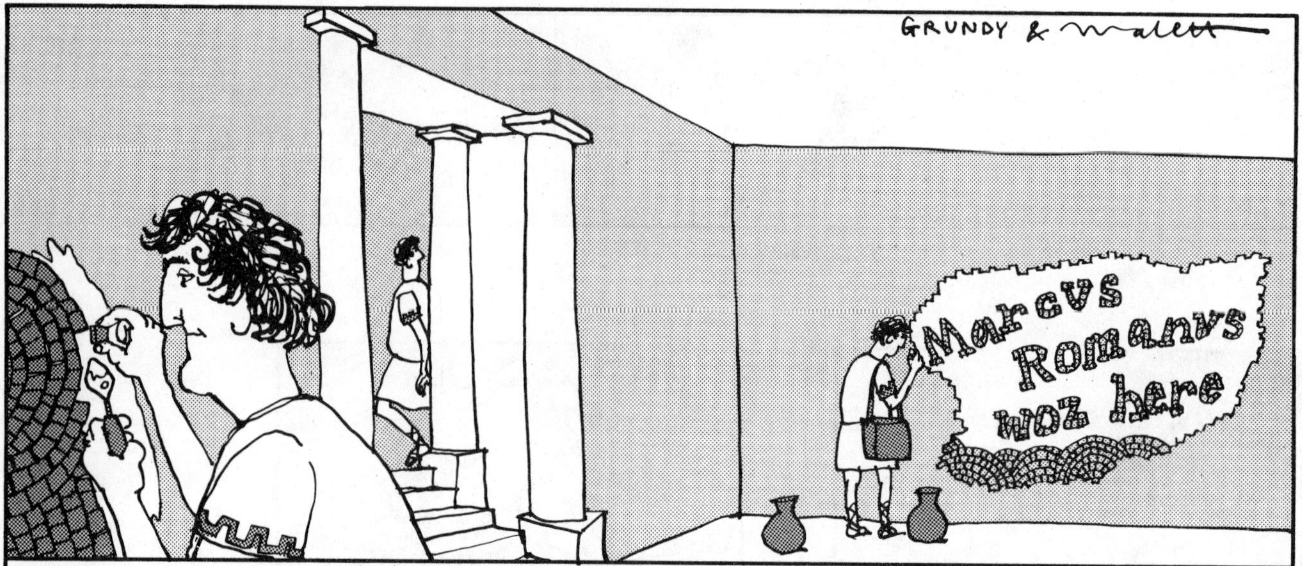
GRUNDY & Malett
Marcvs Romanvs woz here

Graffiti artists of Ancient Rome.

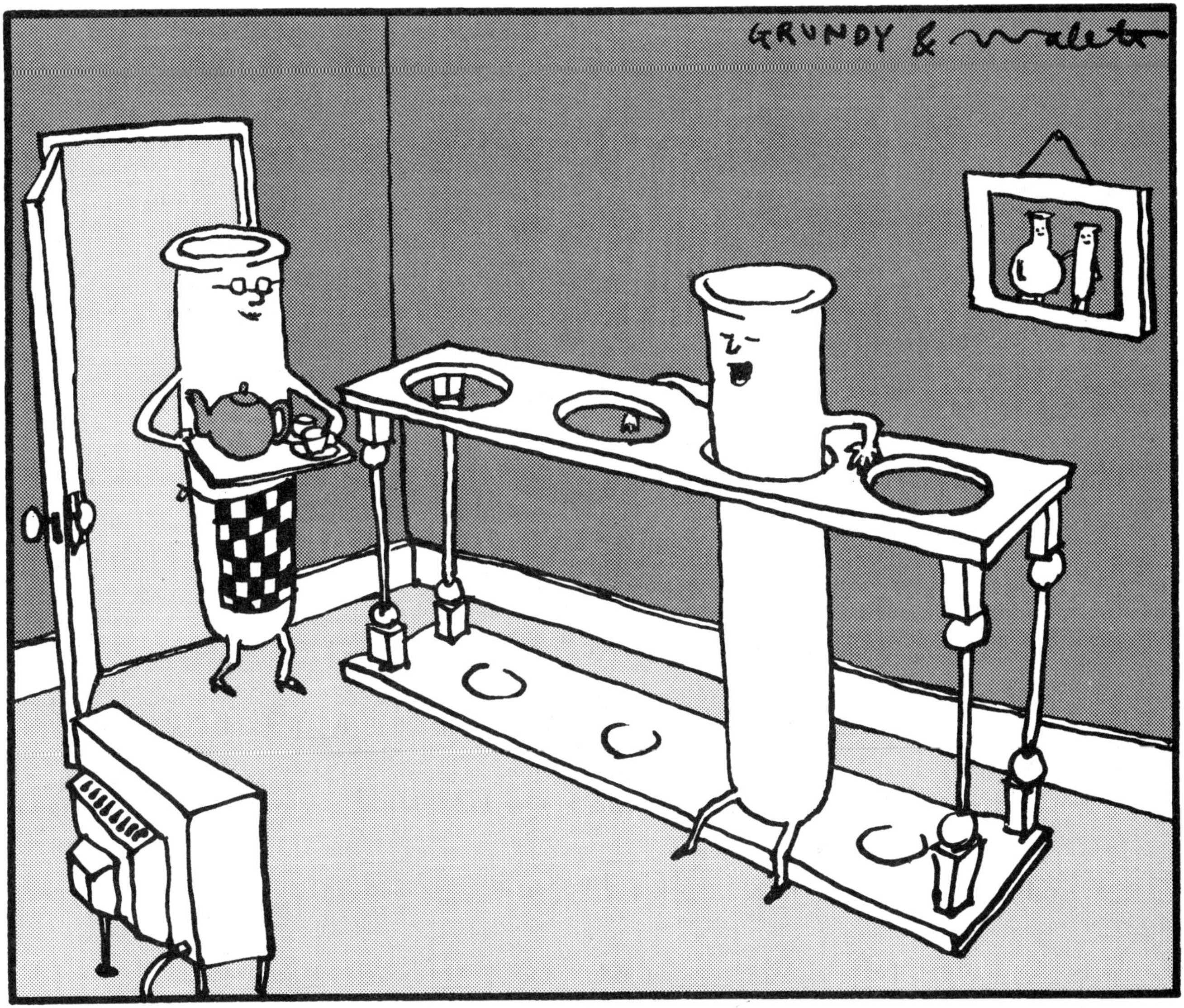
GRUNDY

"Hey, I like the new sofa—very comfy."

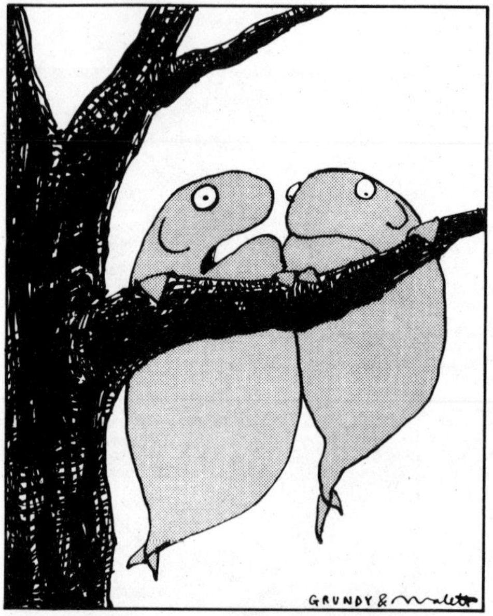
GRUNDY & Malett

"Doris, do you get the feeling we've skipped a few rungs on the evolutionary ladder?"

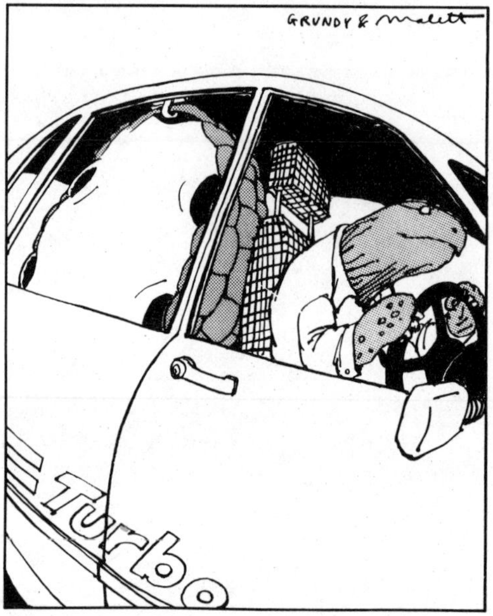
GRUNDY & Malett
Turbo

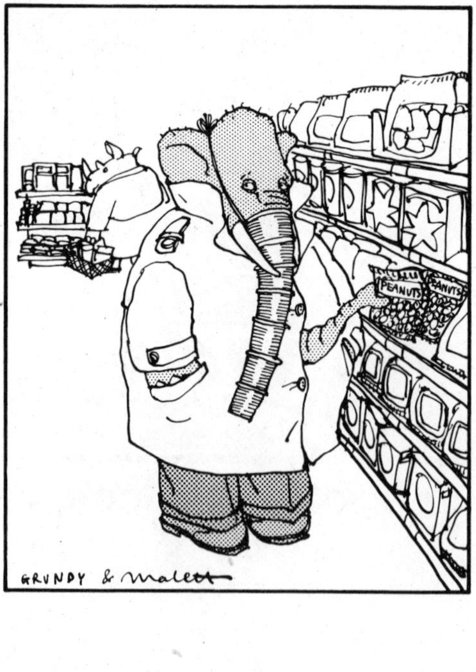
PEANUTS
PEANUTS
GRUNDY & Malett

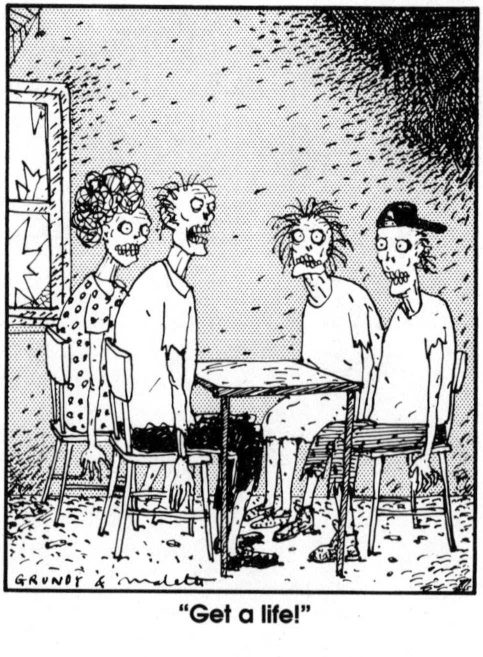
GRUNDY & Malett

"Get a life!"

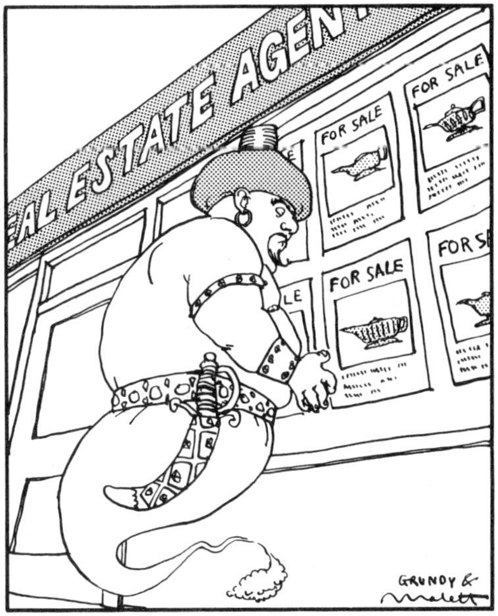
EAL ESTATE AGEN
FOR SALE
FOR SALE
FOR SALE
LE
FOR S
FOR S

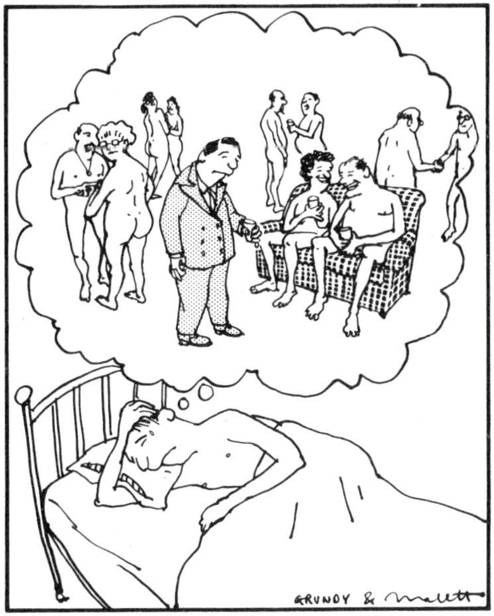

Nudist's nightmare.

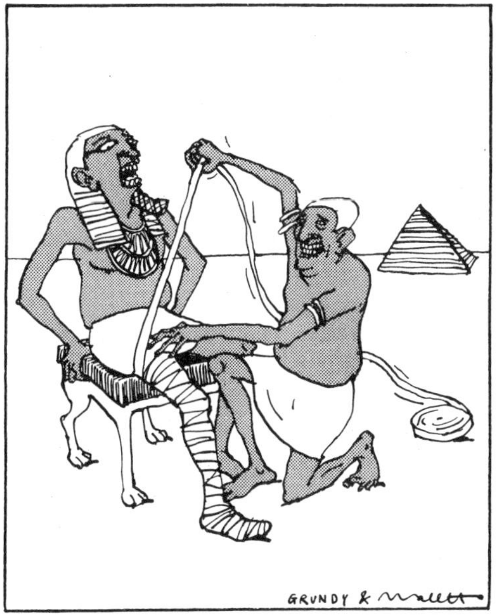

"OK, OK, it's only a sprained ankle.
Let's not get carried away."

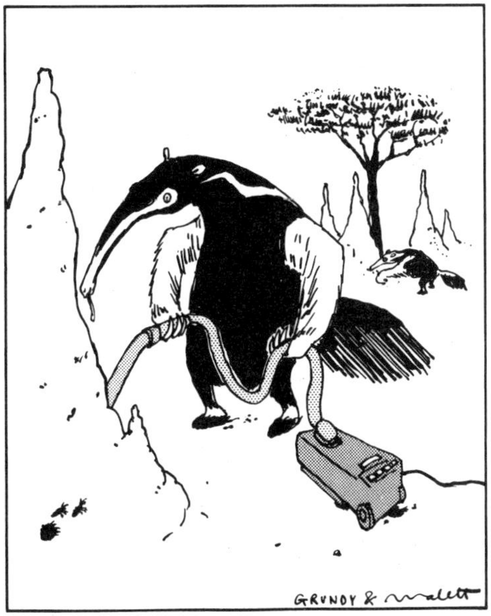

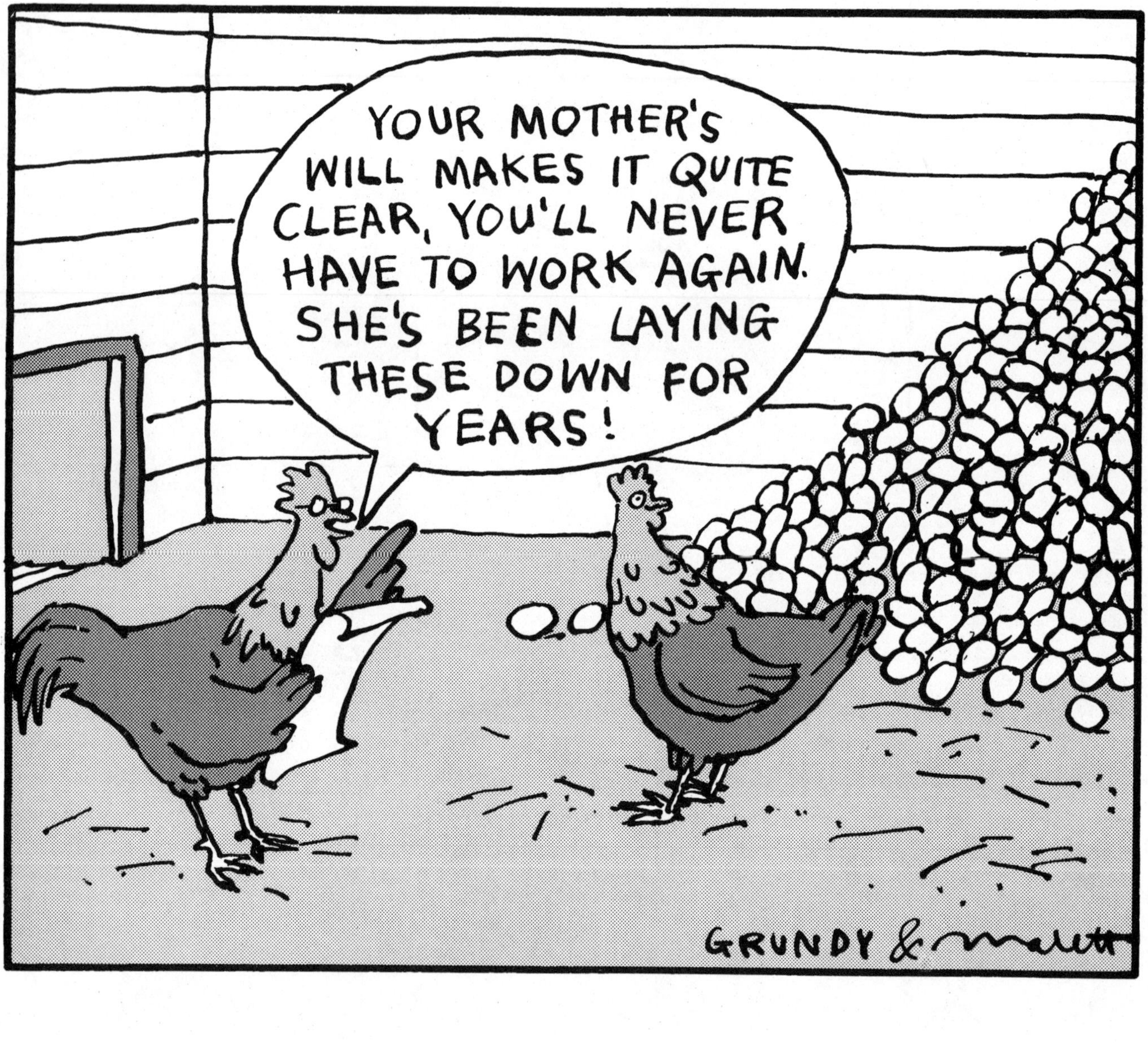
YOUR MOTHER'S WILL MAKES IT QUITE CLEAR, YOU'LL NEVER HAVE TO WORK AGAIN. SHE'S BEEN LAYING THESE DOWN FOR YEARS!
GRUNDY &

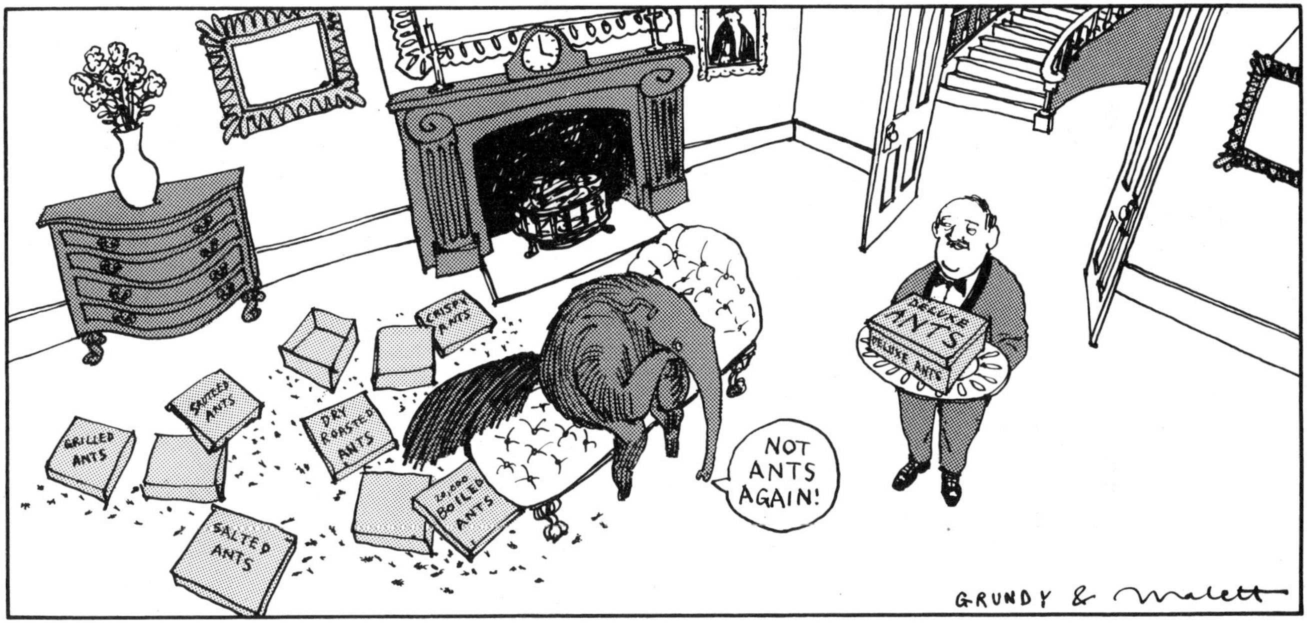
NOT ANTS AGAIN!
DELUXE ANTS
DELUXE ANTS
CRISPY ANTS
SAUTEED ANTS
GRILLED ANTS
DRY ROASTED ANTS
20,000 BOILED ANTS
SALTED ANTS
GRUNDY &

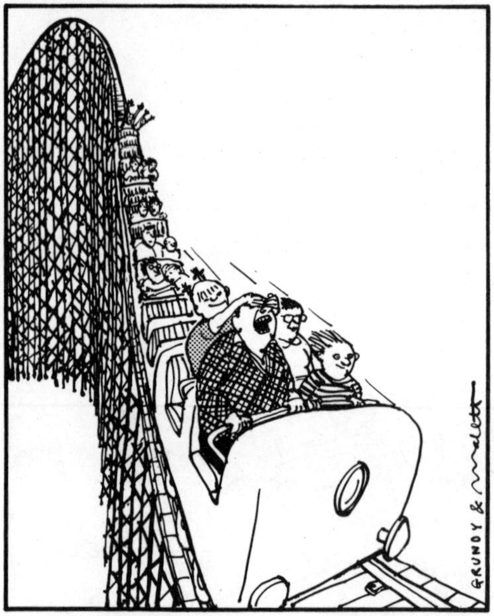
GRUNDY & MALLETT

"For God's sake, Betty! You'll kill us all!"

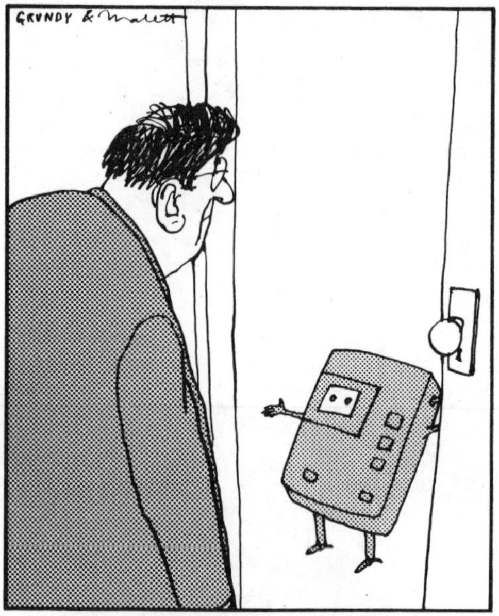
GRUNDY & MALLETT

For two days, all he got was the answering machine—even when he called personally.

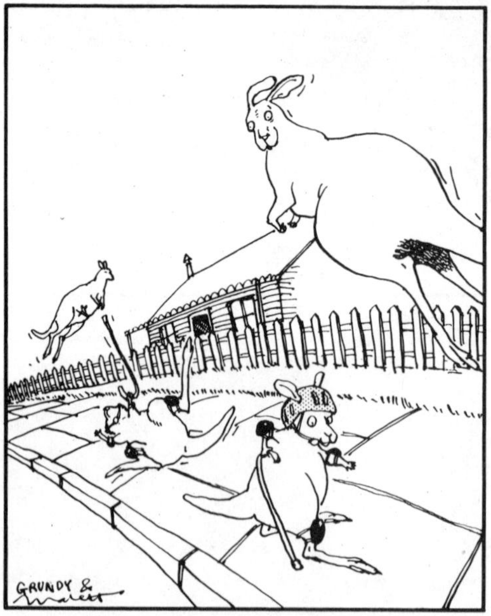
GRUNDY & MALLETT

Walking sticks—the new craze.

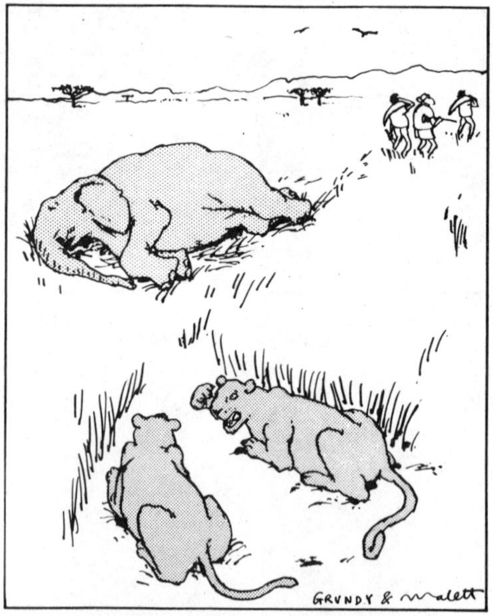
GRUNDY & MALLETT

"Odd, these humans. They leave the meal and take the toothpicks!"

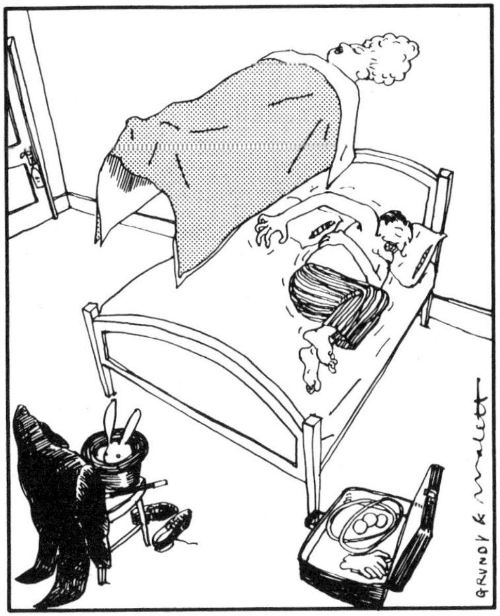
GRUNDY & malett

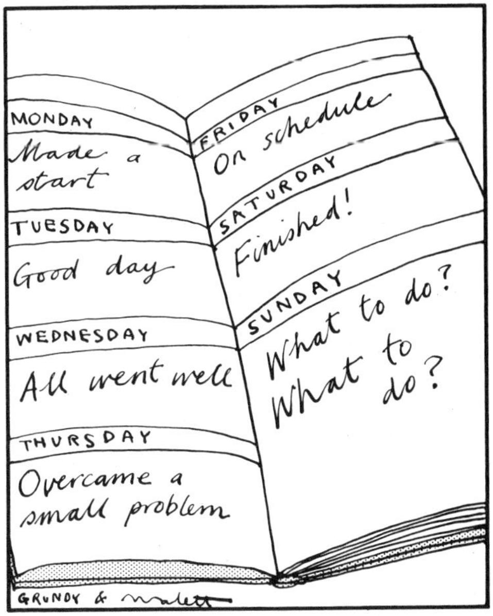
MONDAY
Made a start
TUESDAY
Good day
WEDNESDAY
All went well
THURSDAY
Overcame a small problem
FRIDAY
On schedule
SATURDAY
Finished!
SUNDAY
What to do?
What to do?
GRUNDY & malett

God's diary.

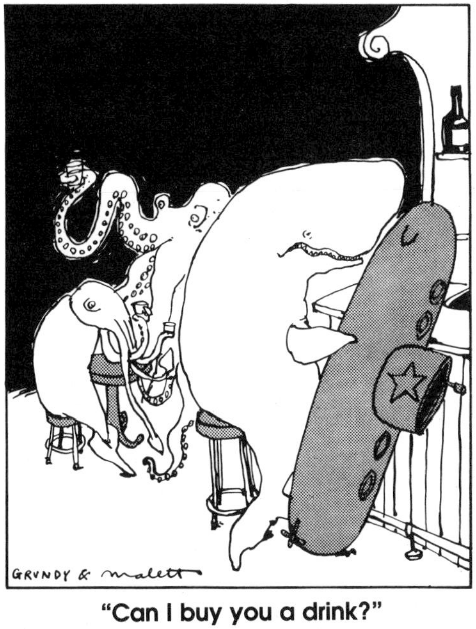
GRUNDY & malett

"Can I buy you a drink?"

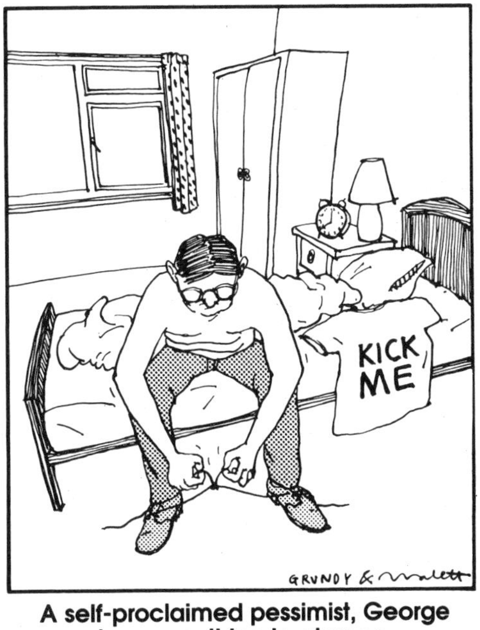
KICK ME
GRUNDY & malett

A self-proclaimed pessimist, George leaves nothing to chance.

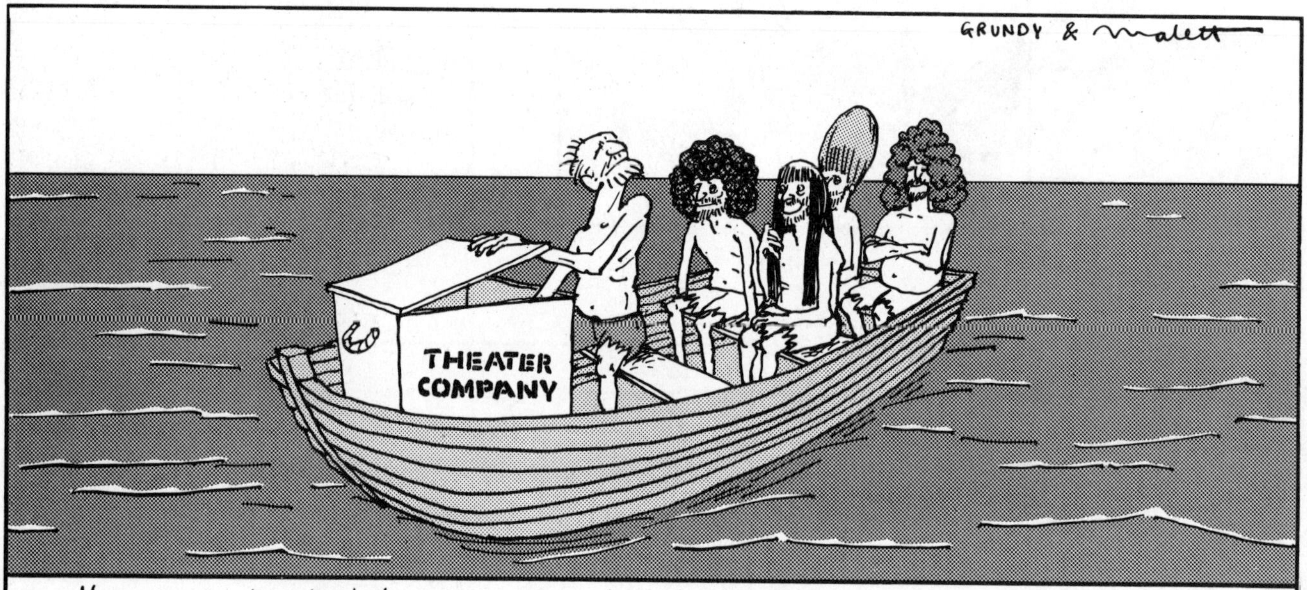
GRUNDY & Malett
THEATER
COMPANY

It was decided that whoever drew the short wig would be thrown overboard.

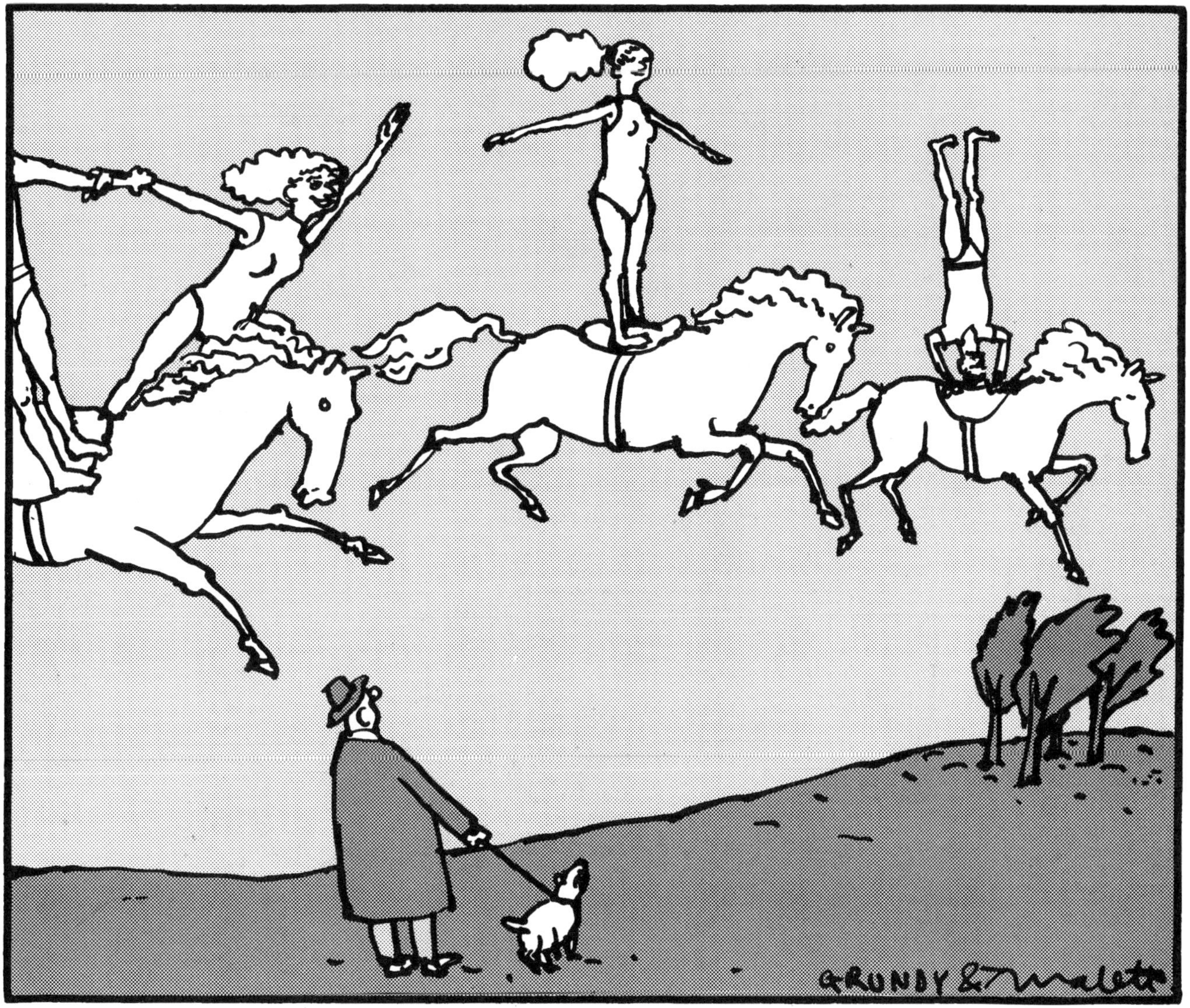
GRUNDY & Maletto

Ghost "trick" riders in the sky.

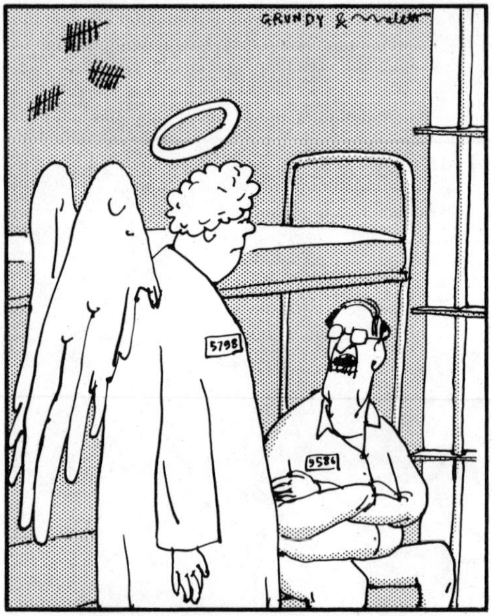
GRUNDY & Malett
5798
5586

"Oh yeah, good story. But we're all innocent in here, pal."

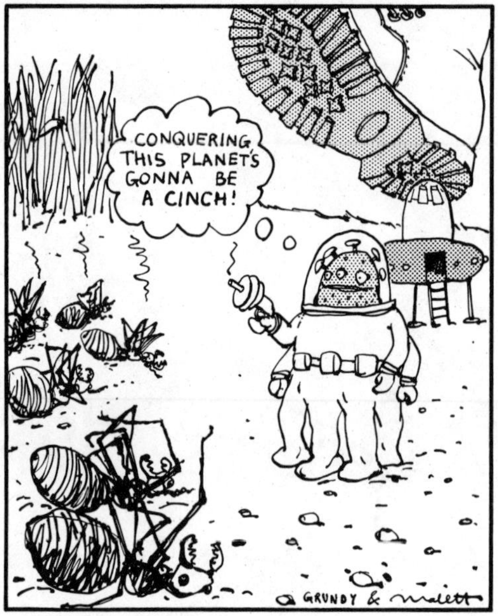
CONQUERING THIS PLANET'S GONNA BE A CINCH!
GRUNDY & Malett

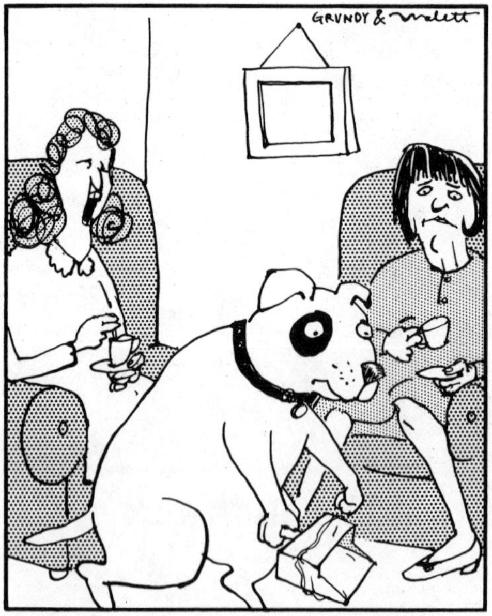
GRUNDY & Malett

"We've *almost* got him house-trained."

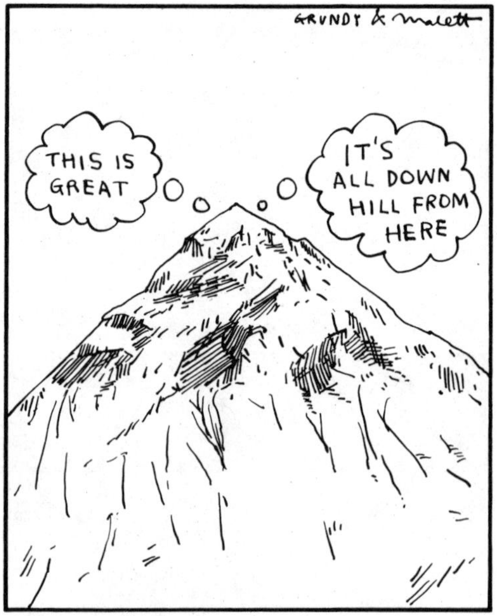
GRUNDY & Malett
THIS IS GREAT
IT'S ALL DOWN HILL FROM HERE

Mount Everest in two minds.

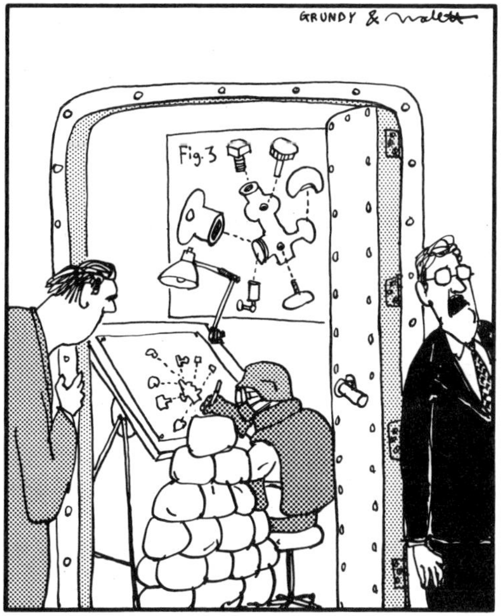
Fig. 3

"... and this is the exploding diagram department."

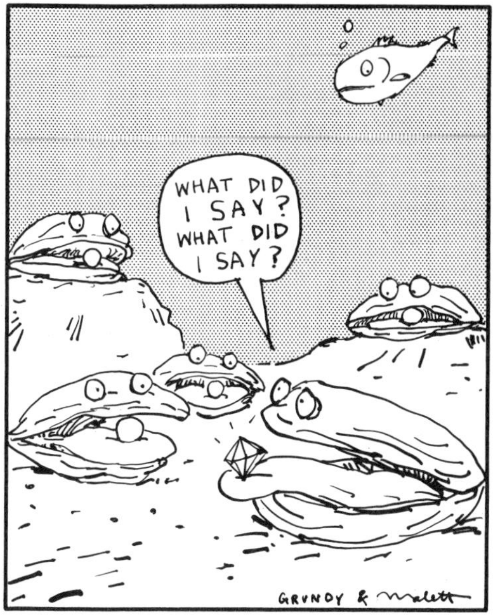
WHAT DID I SAY? WHAT DID I SAY?

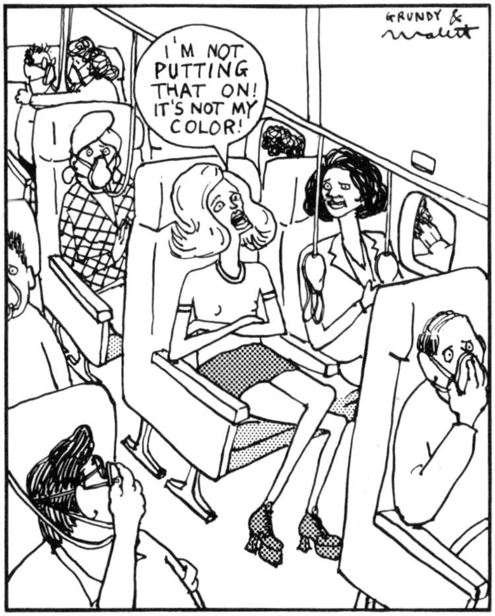
I'M NOT PUTTING THAT ON! IT'S NOT MY COLOR!

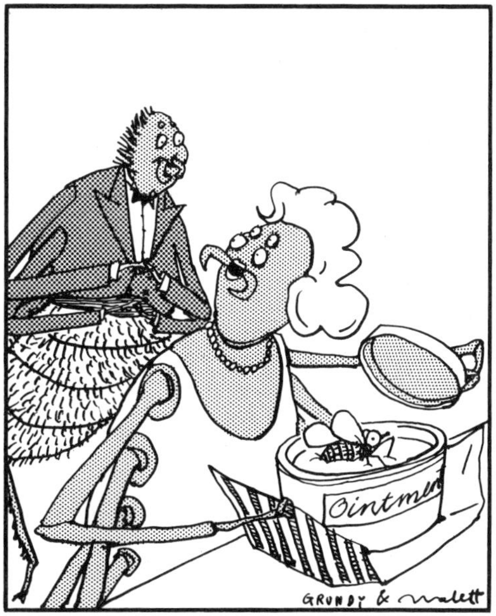

"How thoughtful! You put a fly in the ointment."

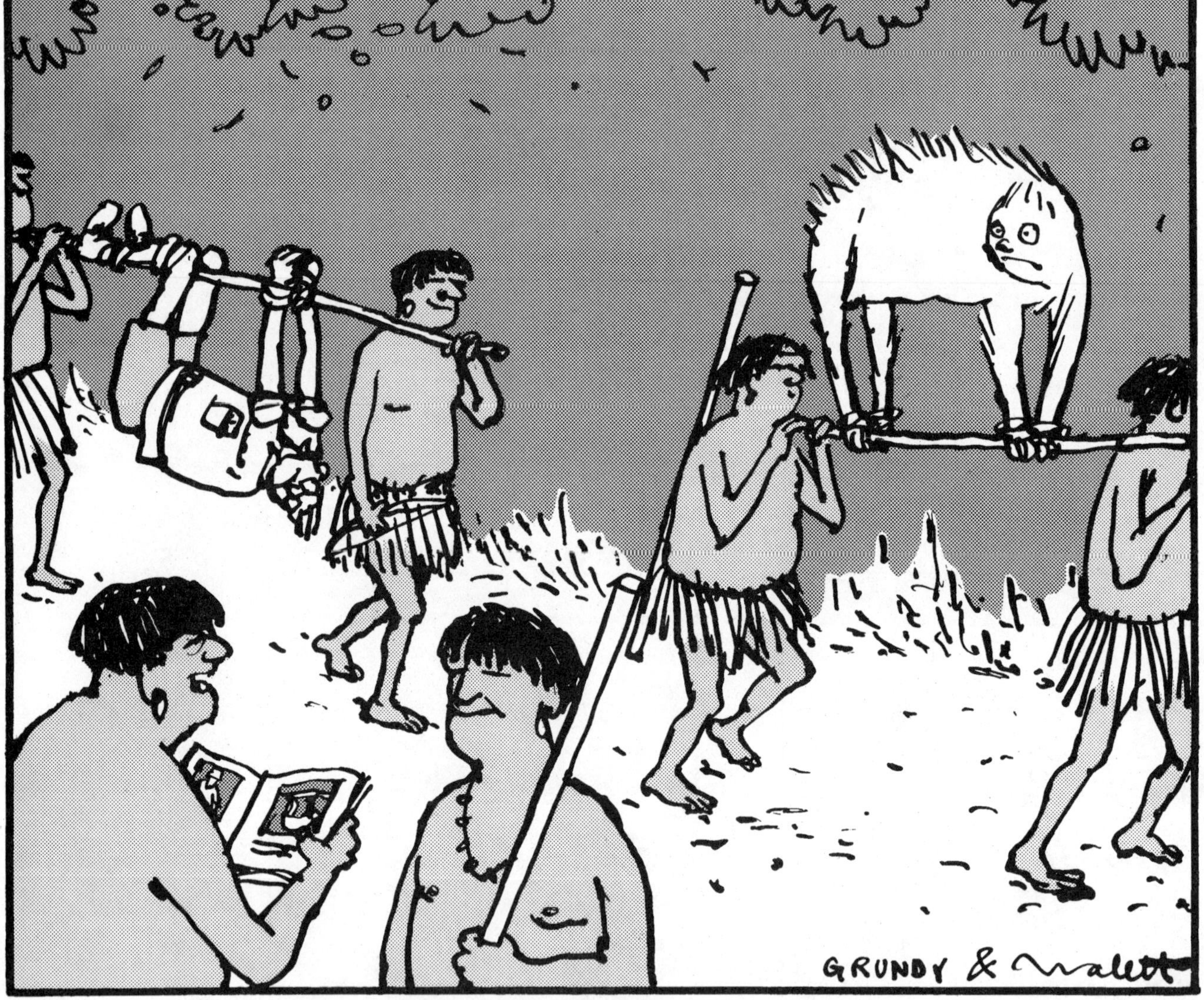
GRUNDY & MALETT

"So today you caught an explorer
and a giant sloth!"

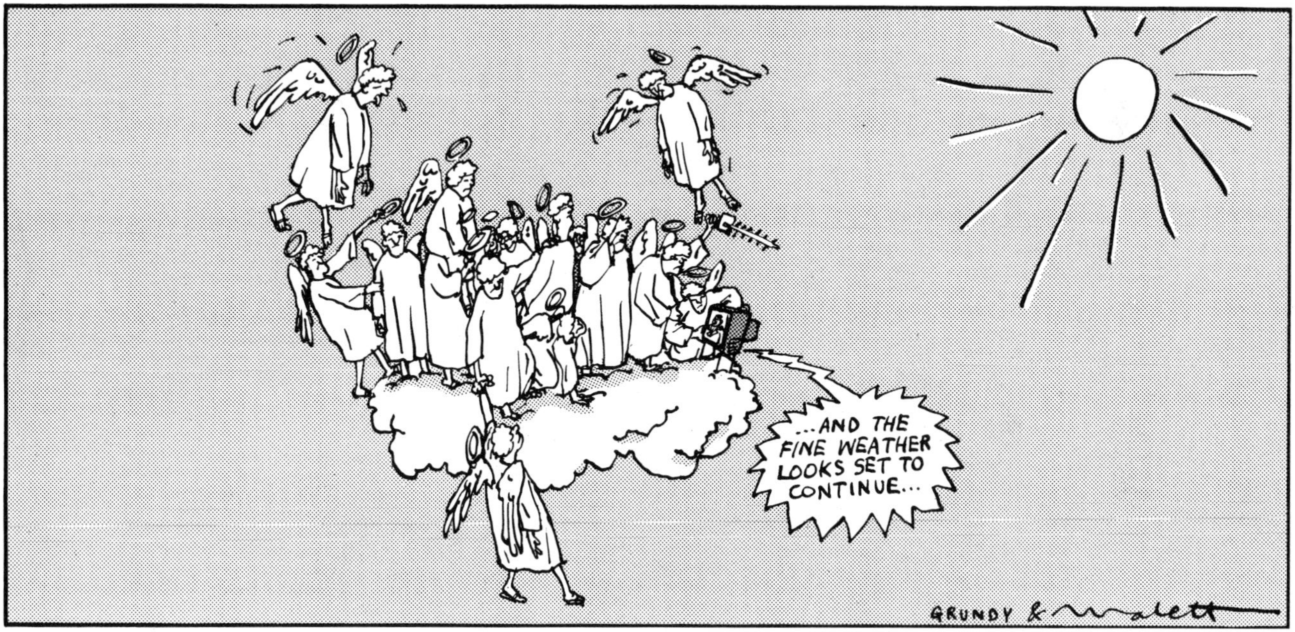
...AND THE FINE WEATHER LOOKS SET TO CONTINUE...
GRUNDY & Malett

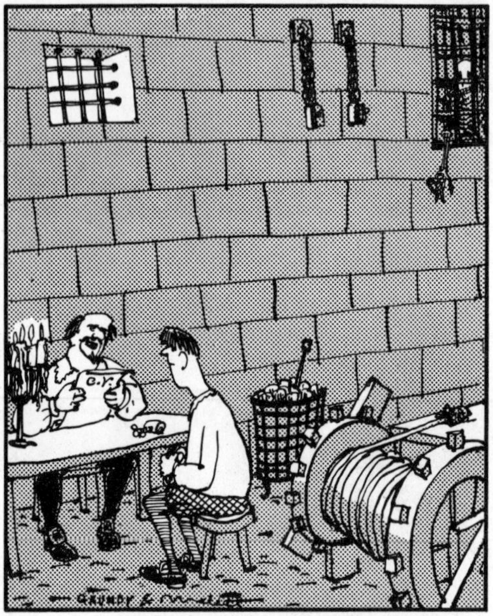
GRUNDY & Malett

"For this job you need a sense of humor."

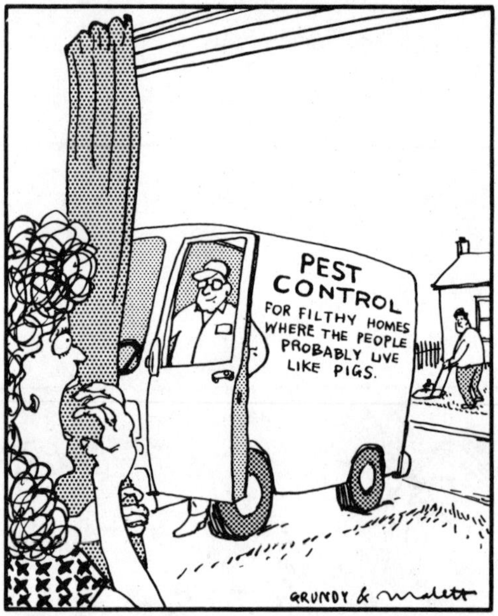
PEST CONTROL
FOR FILTHY HOMES WHERE THE PEOPLE PROBABLY LIVE LIKE PIGS.
GRUNDY & Malett

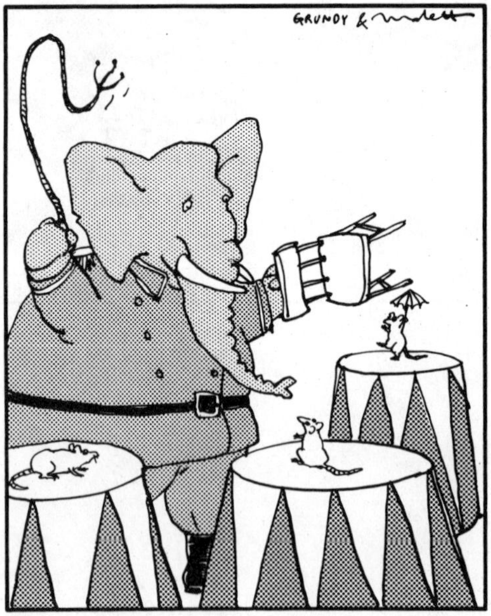
GRUNDY & Malett

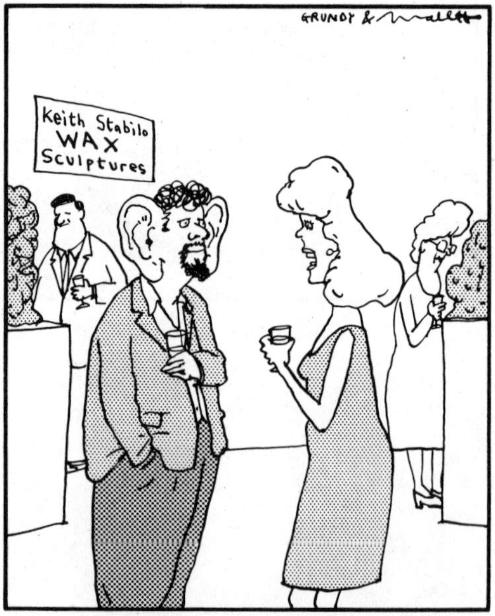
GRUNDY & Malett
Keith Stabilo WAX Sculptures

". . . and if it's not a secret, Mr. Stabilo, where do you get the material to make your sculptures?"

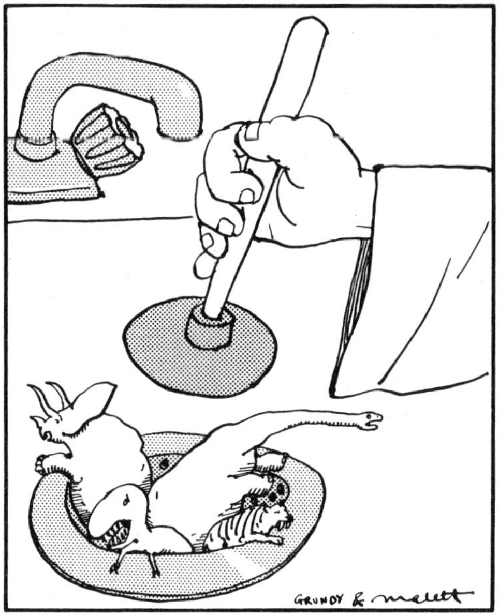

Waste disposal of the gods.

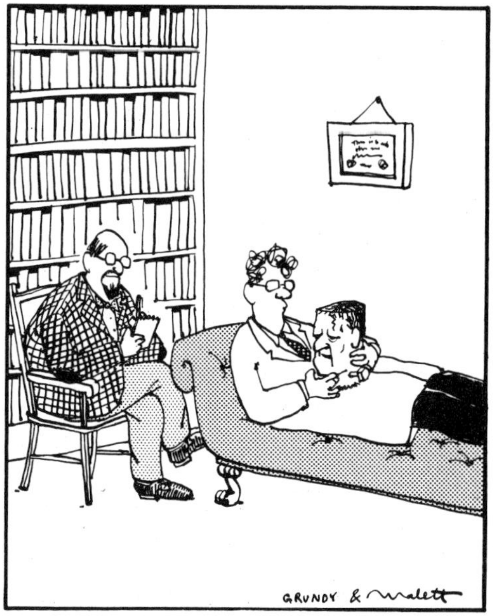

Dr. Frankenstein needs his head examined.

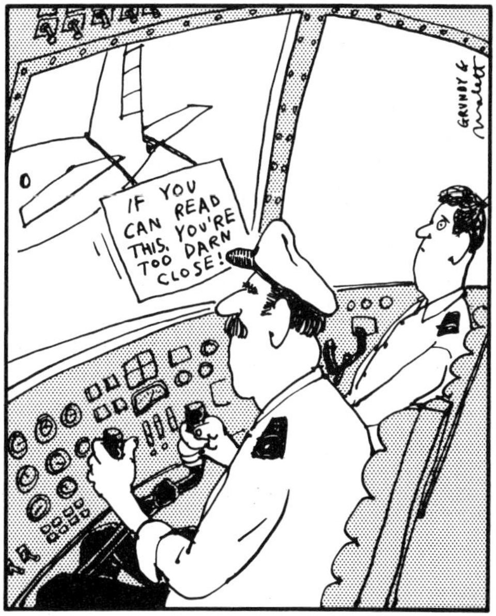
IF YOU CAN READ THIS, YOU'RE TOO DARN CLOSE!

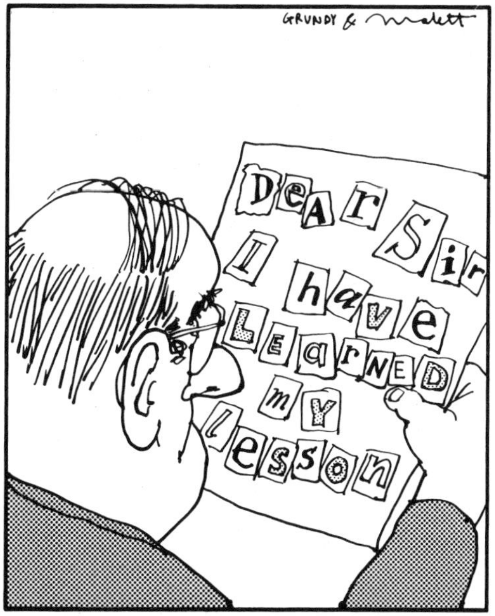
Dear Sir
I have
Learned
my
lesson

A blackmailer's letter to the parole board.

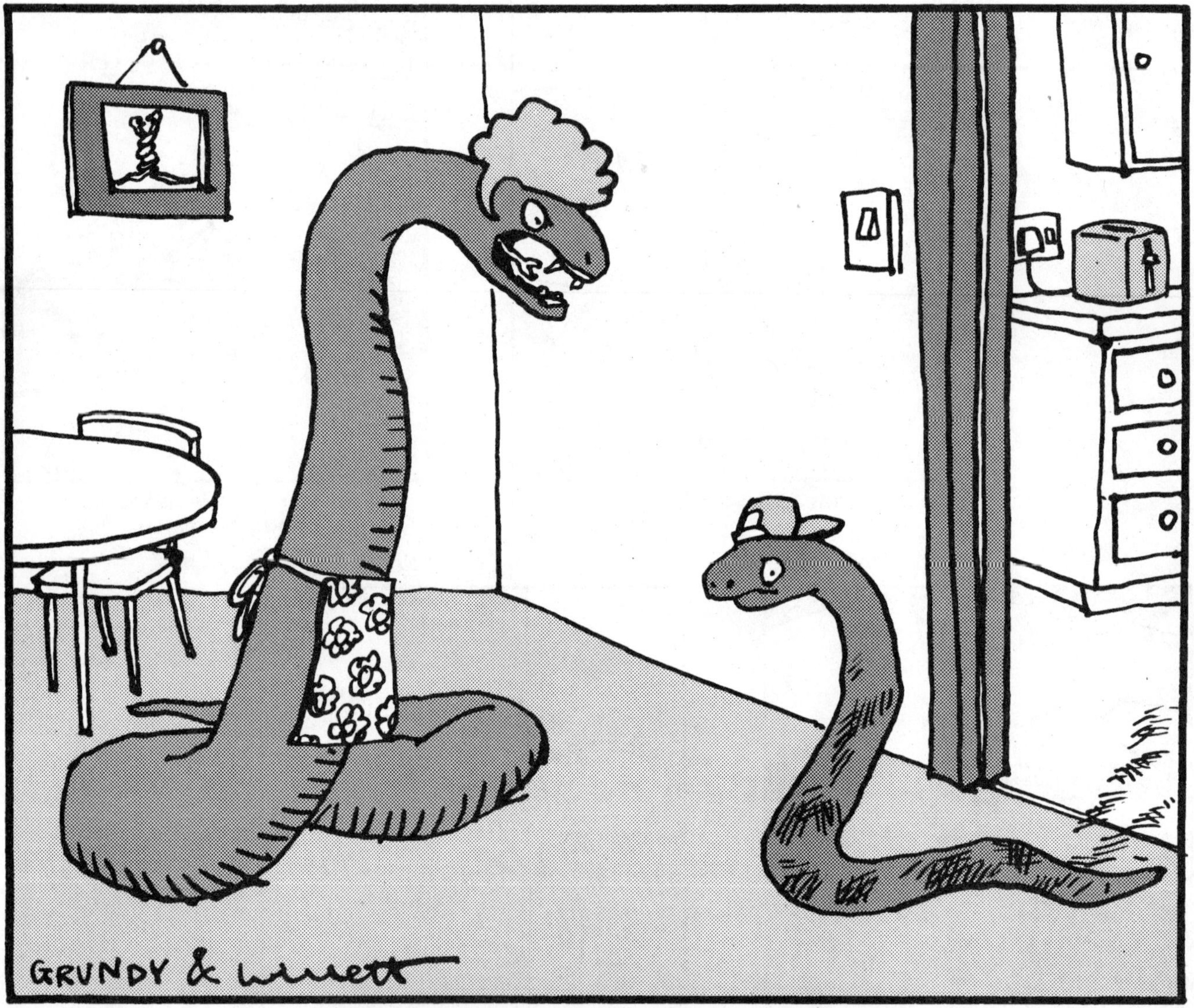
GRUNDY & WILLETT

"Look at the state of you! Molt that skin off immediately!"

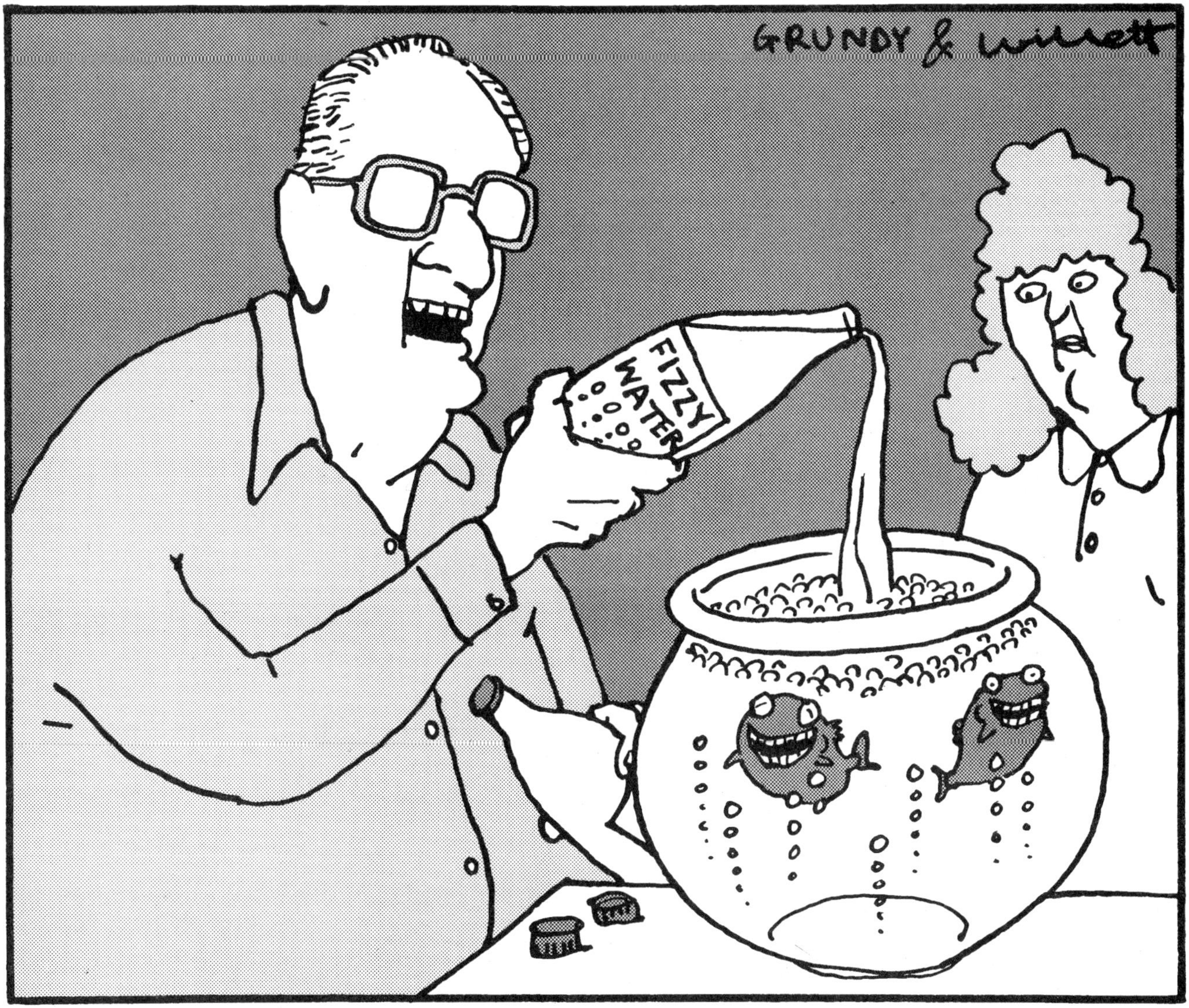
GRUNDY & Willett
FIZZY WATER

"They've been really good, so I'm giving them a bit of a tickle."

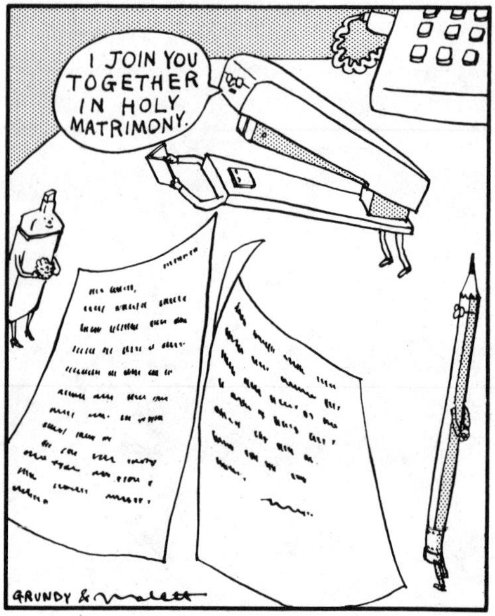
I JOIN YOU TOGETHER IN HOLY MATRIMONY.
GRUNDY & Malett

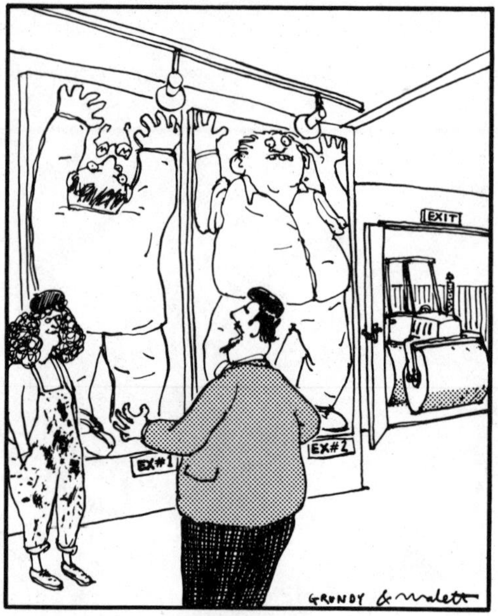
EXIT
EX#1
EX#2
GRUNDY & Malett

". . . and amazingly lifelike!"

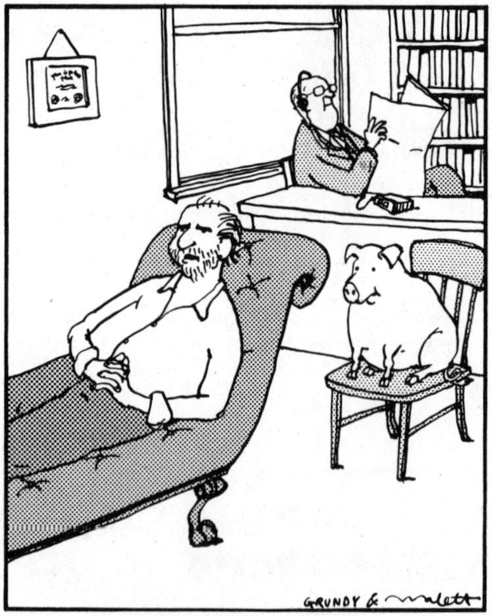
GRUNDY & Malett

Dr. Corder had trained Pinky to grunt in all the right places.

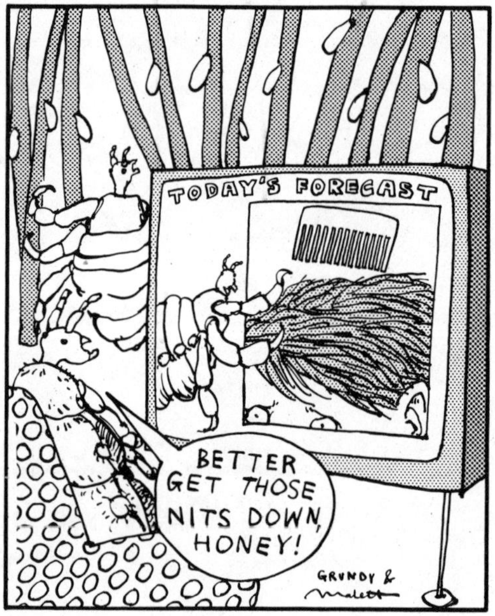
TODAY'S FORECAST
BETTER GET THOSE NITS DOWN, HONEY!
GRUNDY & Malett

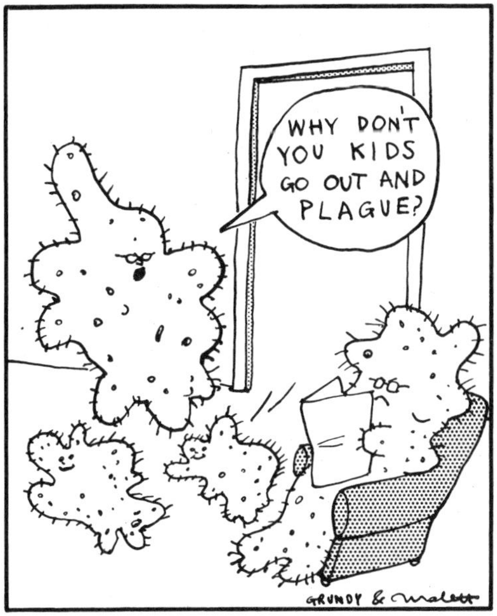
WHY DON'T YOU KIDS GO OUT AND PLAGUE?
GRUNDY & MALETT

The germ family at home.

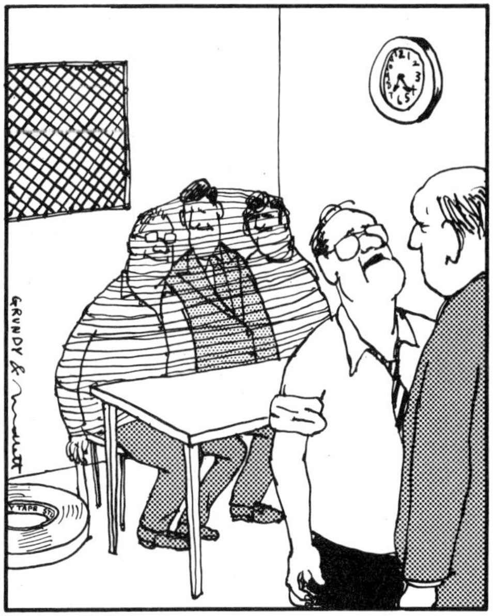
GRUNDY & MALETT

"This could be a problem, Captain. Looks like they're sticking together."

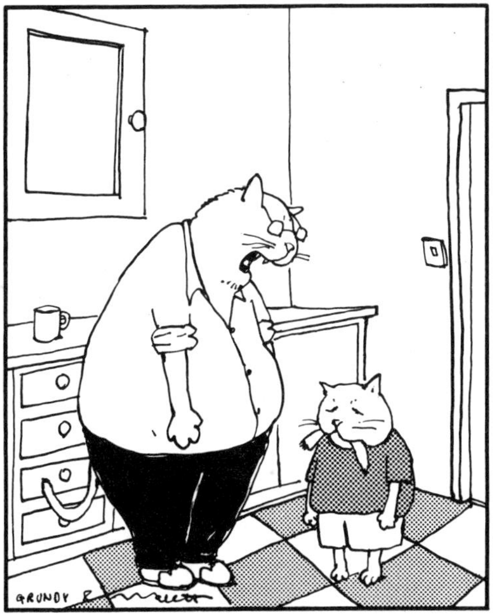
GRUNDY & MALETT

"It's OK to chase your tail, son. Just try not to catch it."

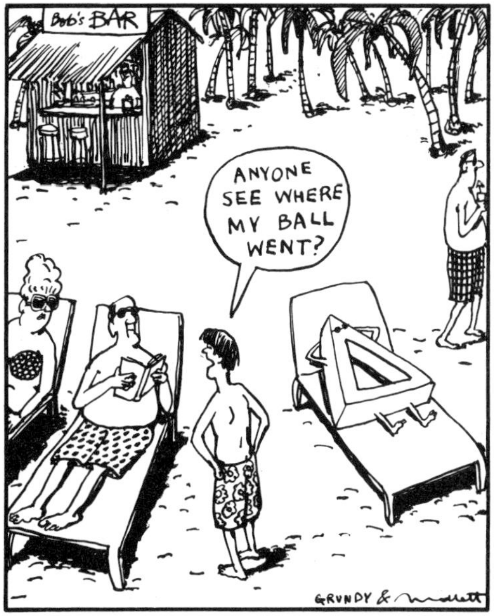
Bob's BAR
ANYONE SEE WHERE MY BALL WENT?
GRUNDY & MALETT

Meanwhile, in Bermuda . . .

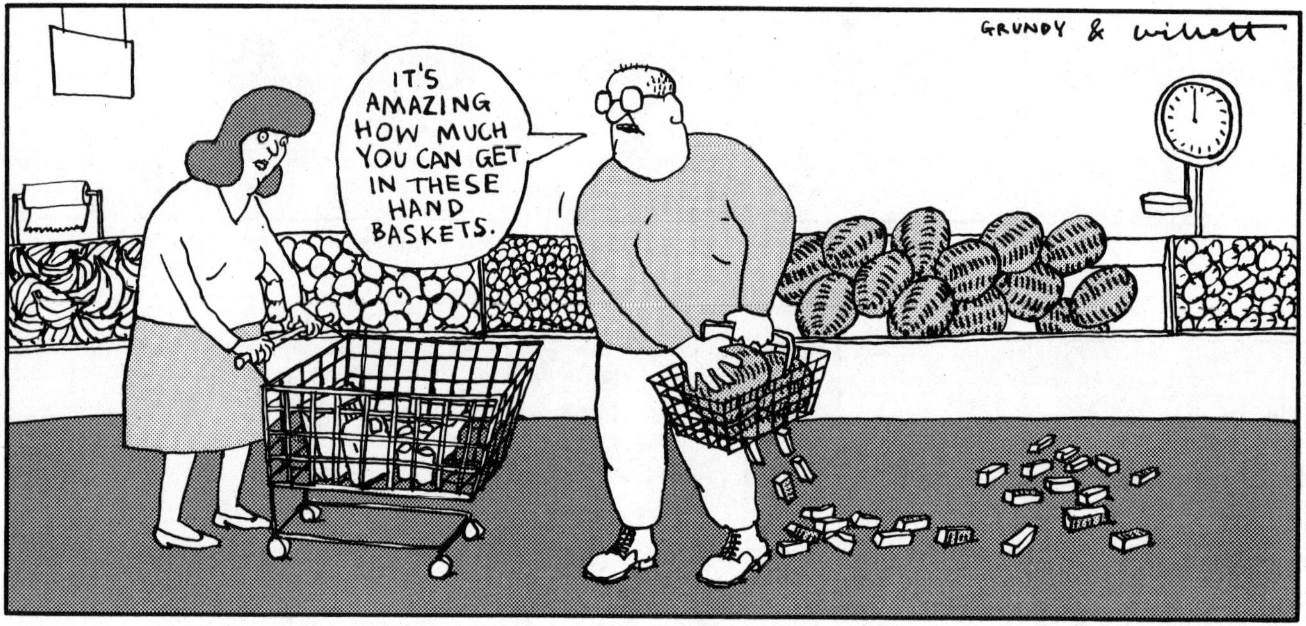
GRUNDY & willett
IT'S AMAZING HOW MUCH YOU CAN GET IN THESE HAND BASKETS.

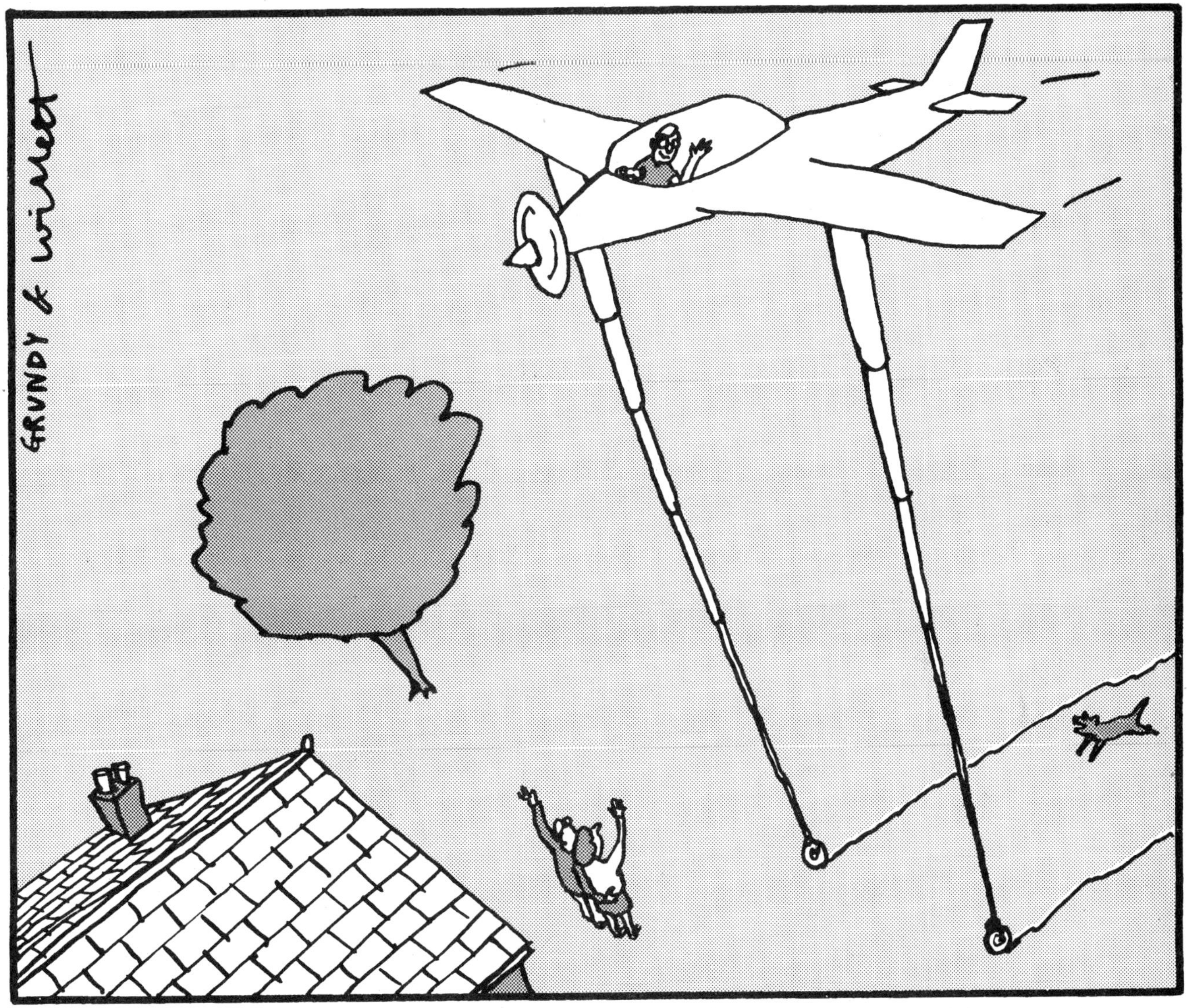
GRUNDY & Willett

Jeff's first plane had stabilizers.

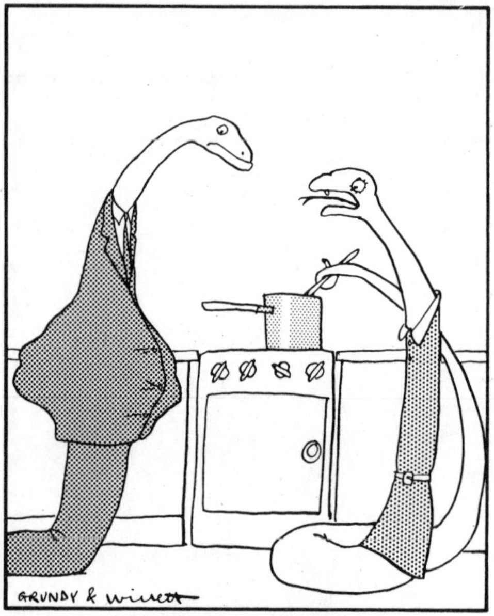
GRUNDY & WILLETT

"Why didn't you tell me you already had dinner?"

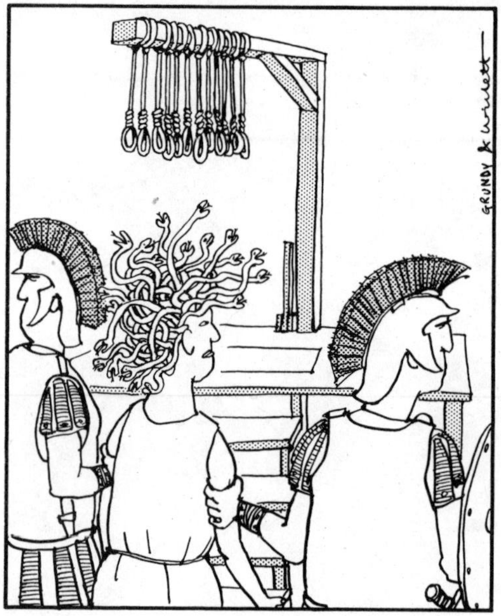
GRUNDY & WILLETT

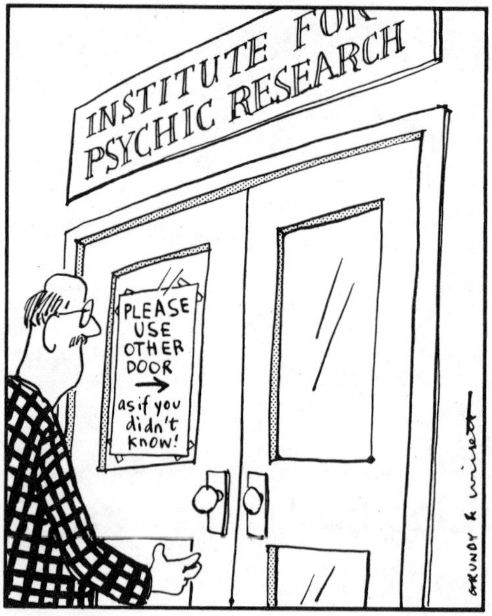
INSTITUTE FOR PSYCHIC RESEARCH
PLEASE USE OTHER DOOR →
as if you didn't know!
GRUNDY & WILLETT

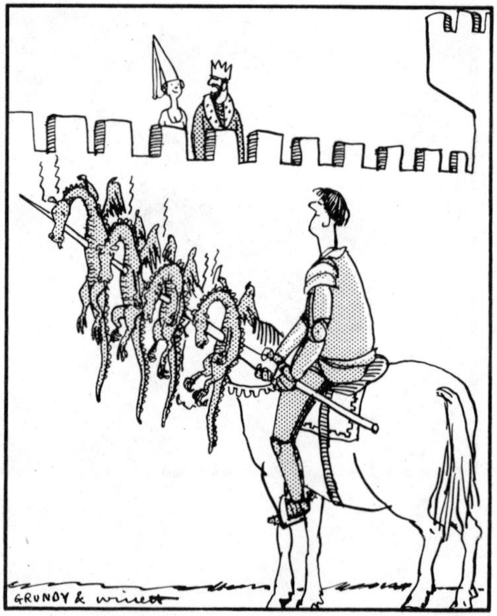
GRUNDY & WILLETT

"I'll say this for him, what he lacks in quality, he makes up in quantity."

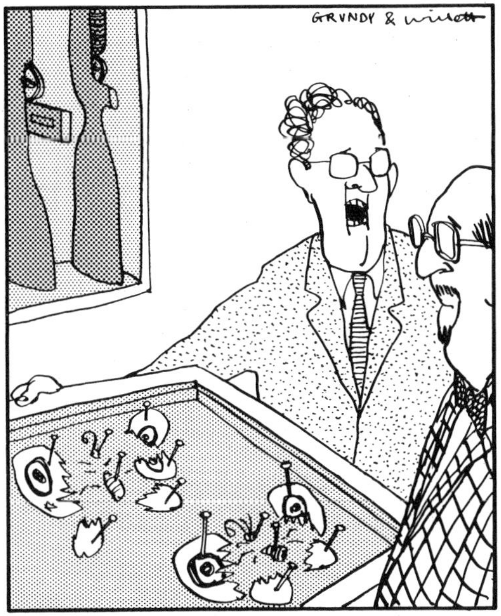
GRUNDY & WILLETT

"A net? . . . Never thought of that."

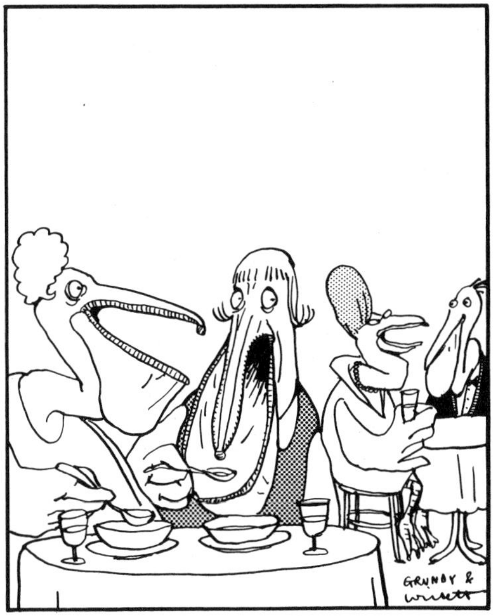
GRUNDY & WILLETT

"Don't look now, but guess who's had a beak job."

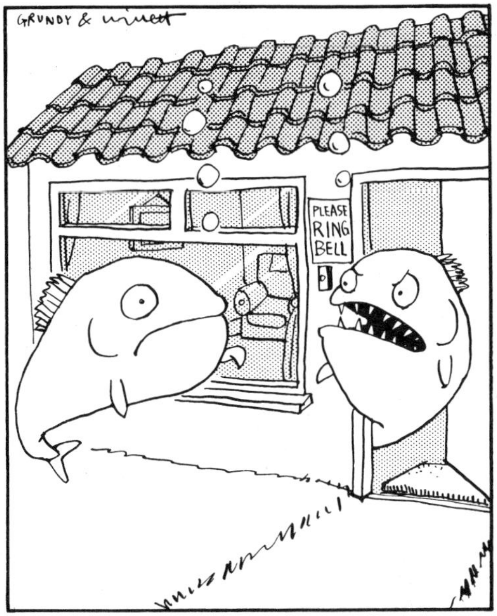
GRUNDY & WILLETT
PLEASE RING BELL

"I've told you before—
DON'T TAP ON THE GLASS!"

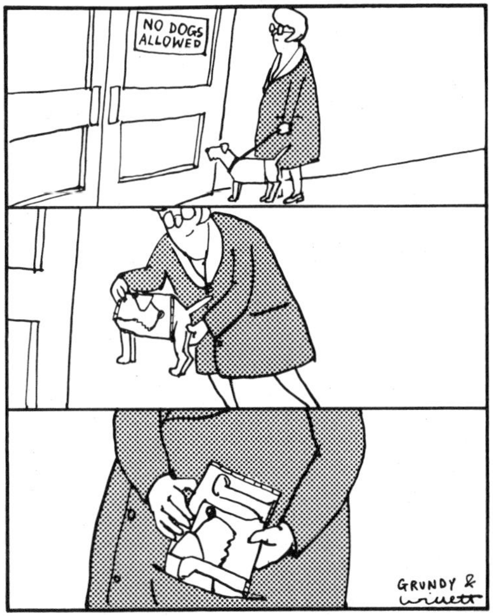
NO DOGS ALLOWED
GRUNDY & WILLETT

Breeders perfect the foldaway dog.

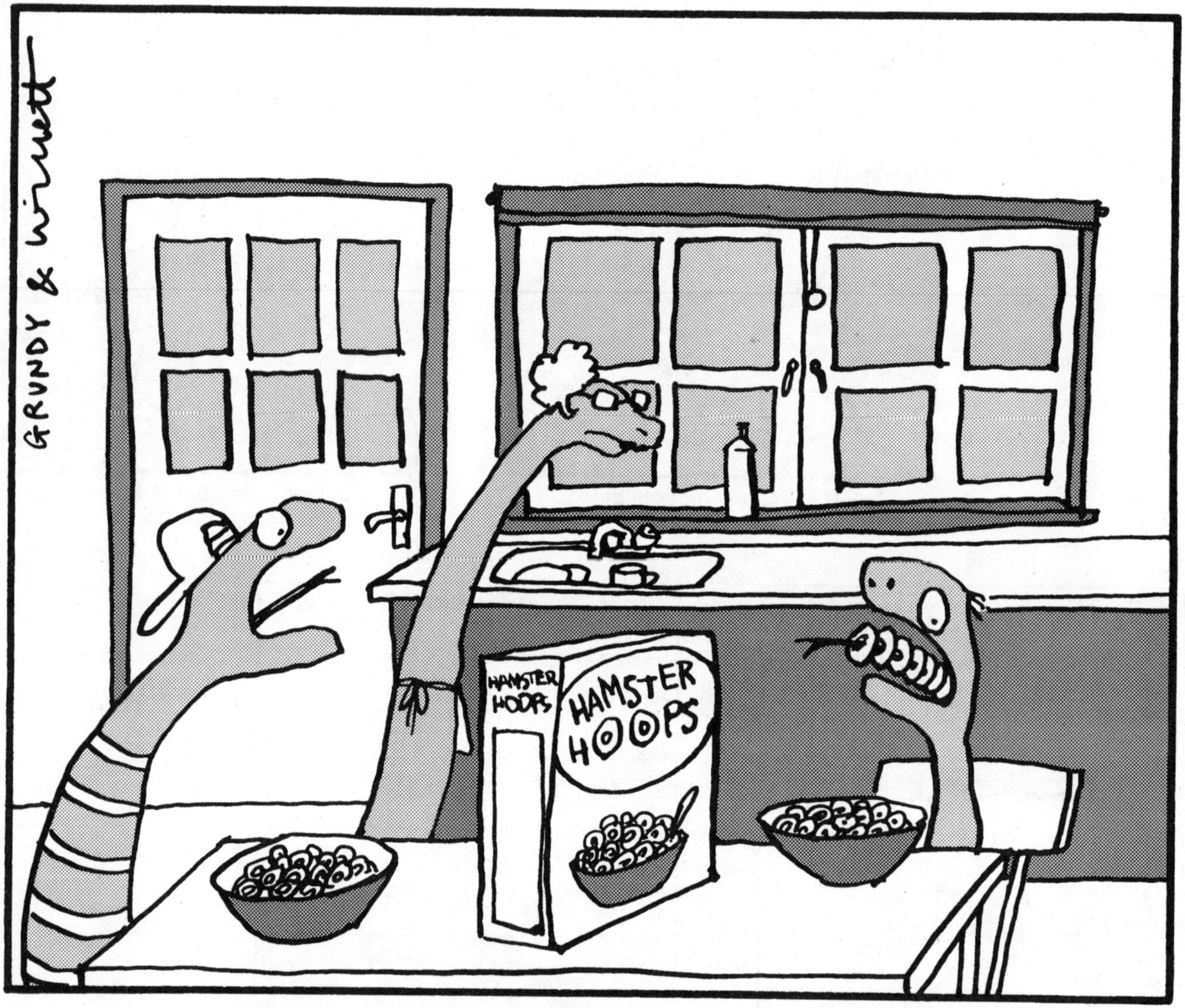
GRUNDY & Willett
HAMSTER HOOPS
HAMSTER HOOPS

"Mom, Bobby can't swallow his cereal!"

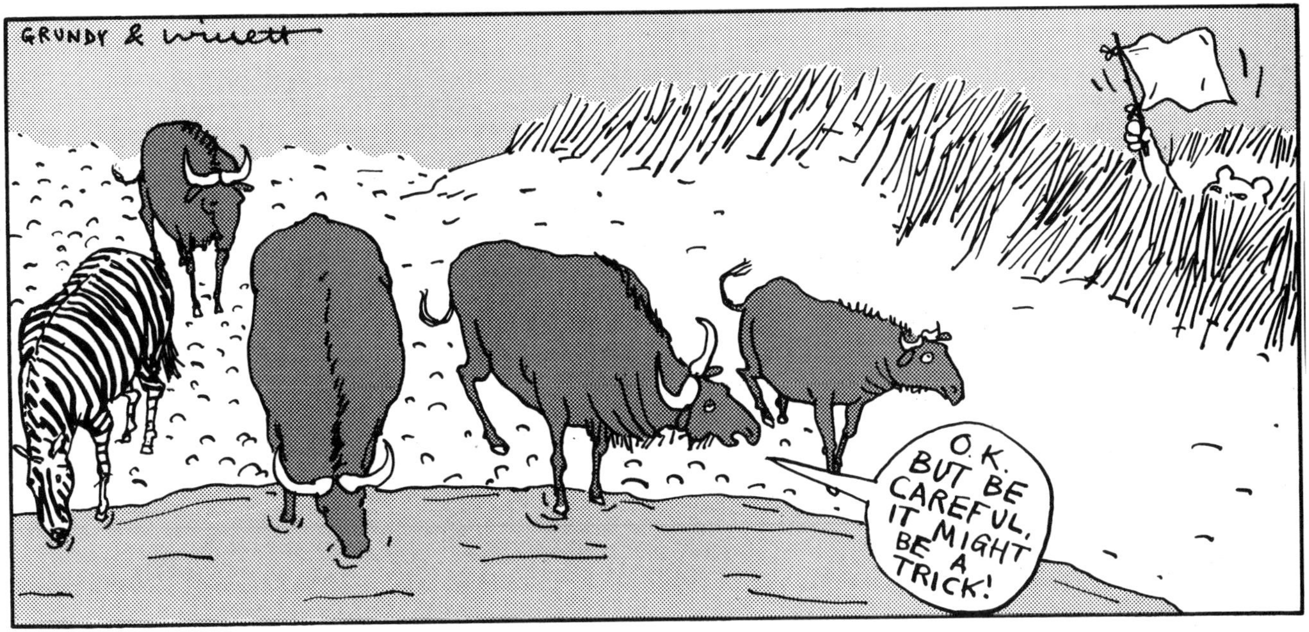
GRUNDY & WILLETT
O.K. BUT BE CAREFUL, IT MIGHT BE A TRICK!

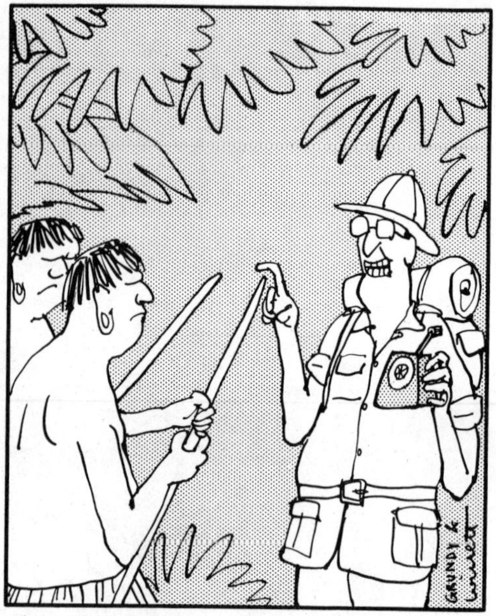
GRUNDY & WILLETT

Pencil sharpener salesman and explorer
Reg Payne seals his own fate.

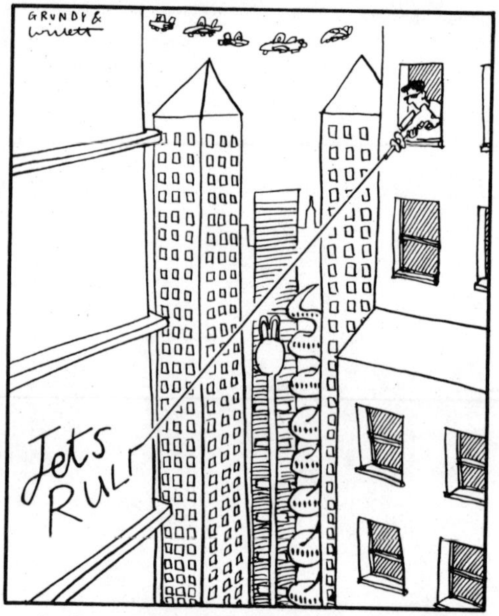
GRUNDY & WILLETT
Jets RUL

In the year 2040, graffiti laser artists
are impossible to catch.

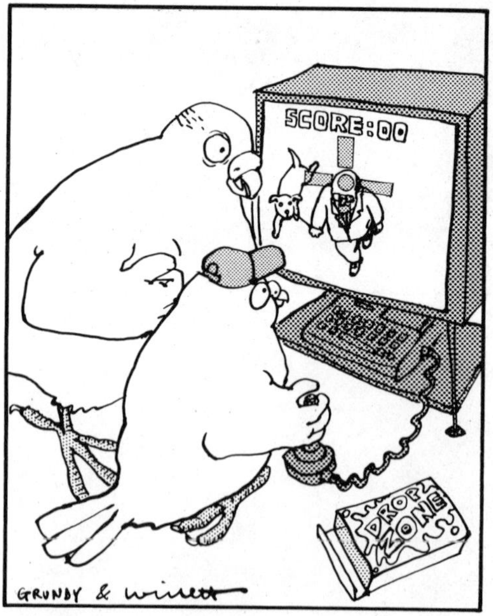
SCORE:00
DROP ZONE
GRUNDY & WILLETT

"OK, son . . . steady, steady . . . now!"

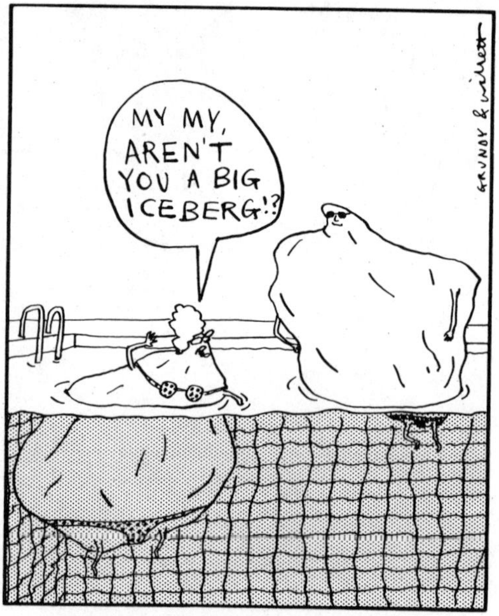
GRUNDY & WILLETT
MY MY, AREN'T YOU A BIG ICEBERG!?

Hilda is in for a big disappointment.

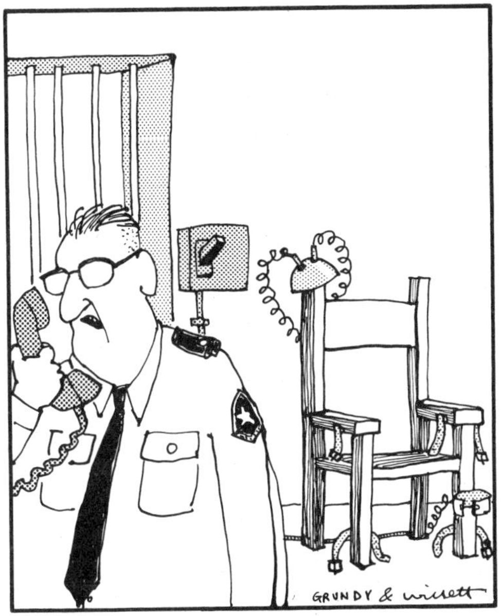
GRUNDY & willett

"I know it's got a lifetime guarantee, but whose lifetime?"

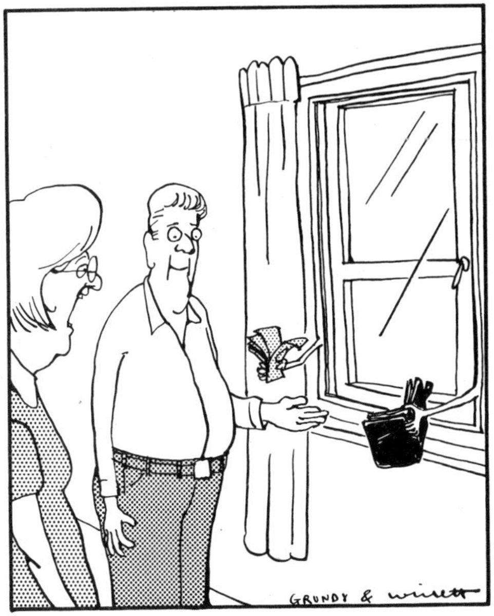
GRUNDY & willett

Just as the salesman had said, after five years the Claymans' double-glazing paid for itself.

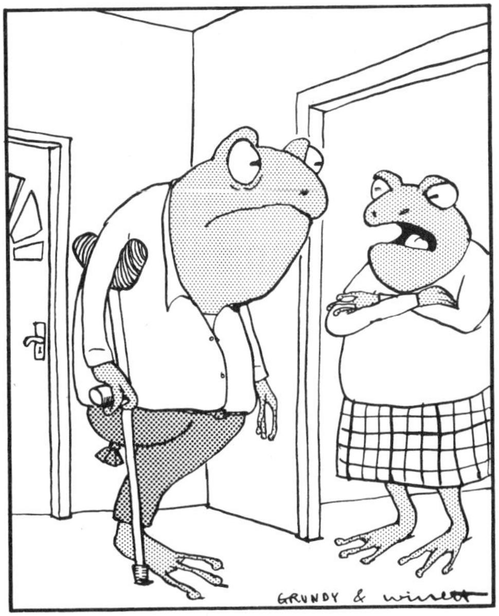
GRUNDY & willett

"So you finally had to do it! You've been to that restaurant raising money for your gambling debts, haven't you?"

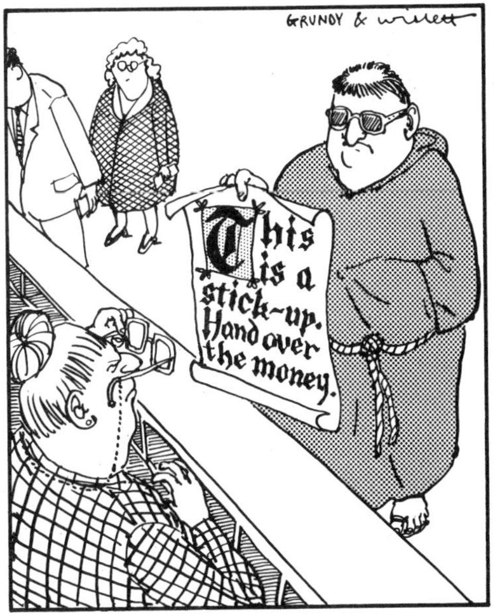
GRUNDY & willett
This is a stick-up. Hand over the money.

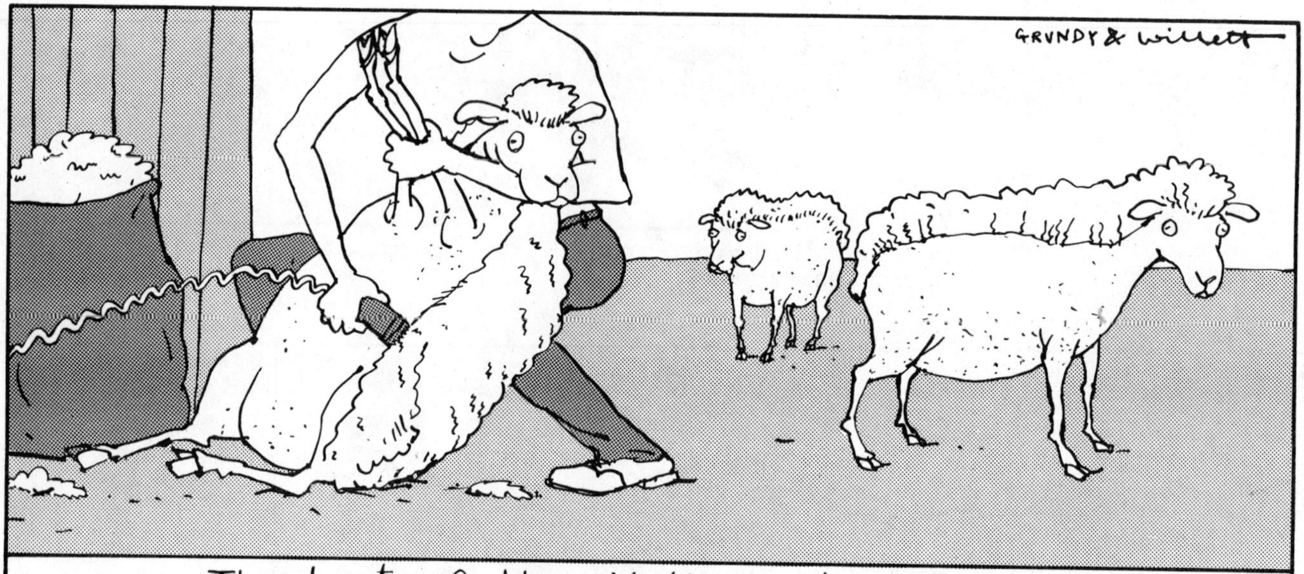
GRUNDY & Willett

The Last of the Mohican sheep-shearers.

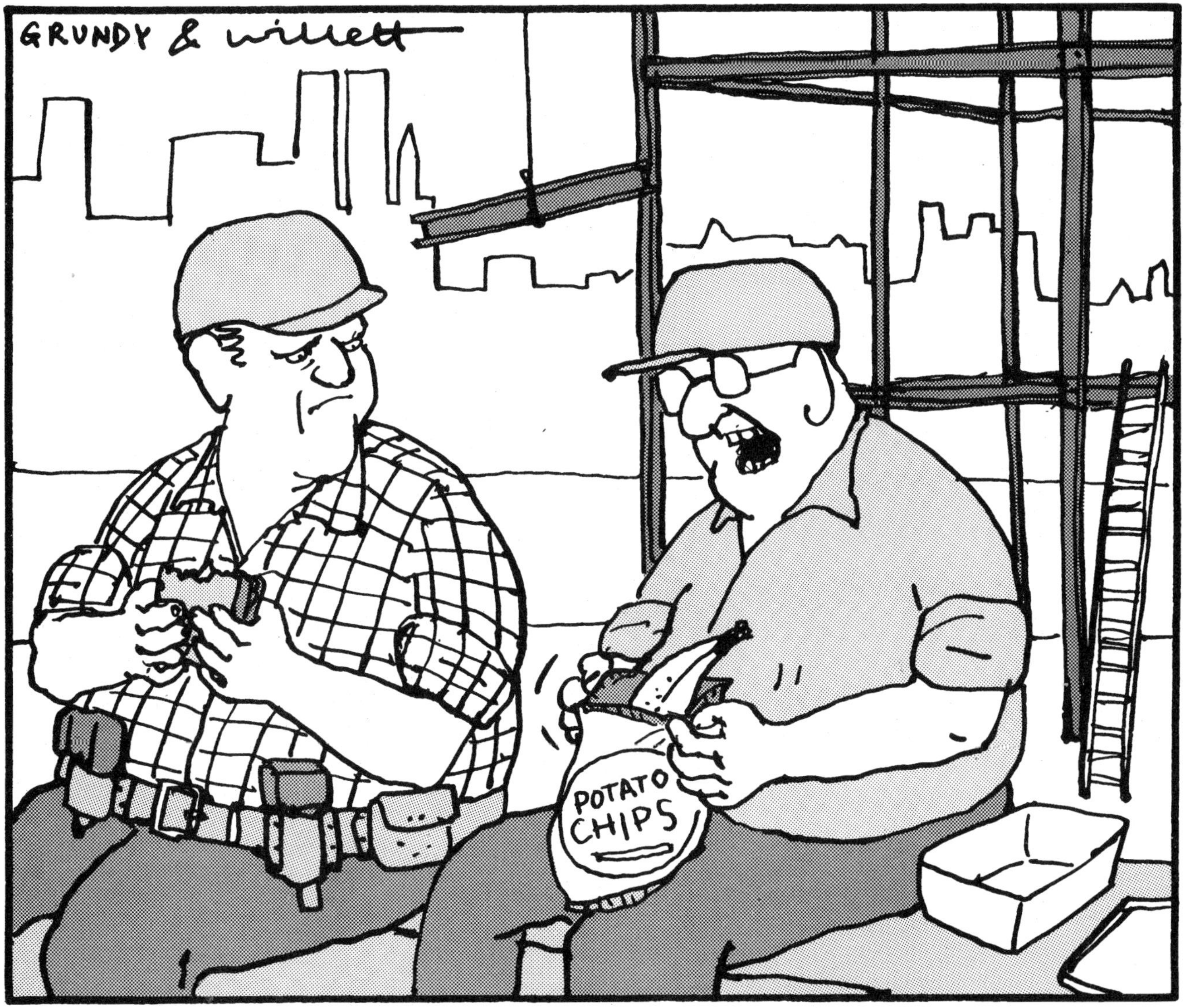
GRUNDY & willett
POTATO
CHIPS

"My wife likes to surprise me."

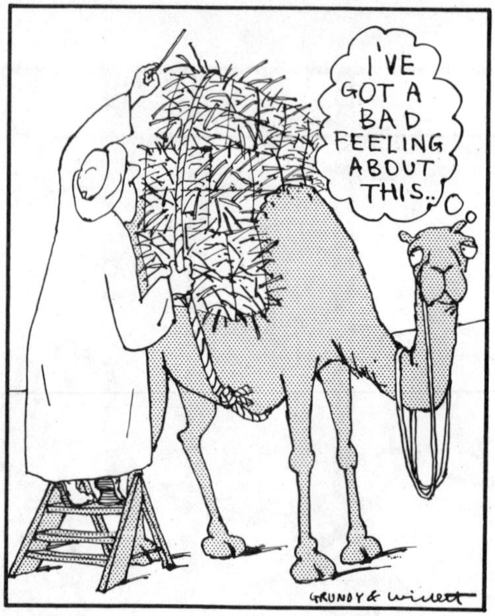
I'VE GOT A BAD FEELING ABOUT THIS..
GRUNDY & WILLETT

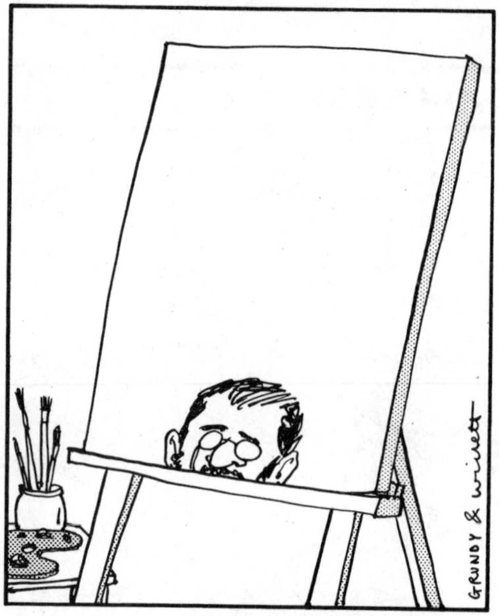
GRUNDY & WILLETT

Toulouse-Lautrec's self-portrait.

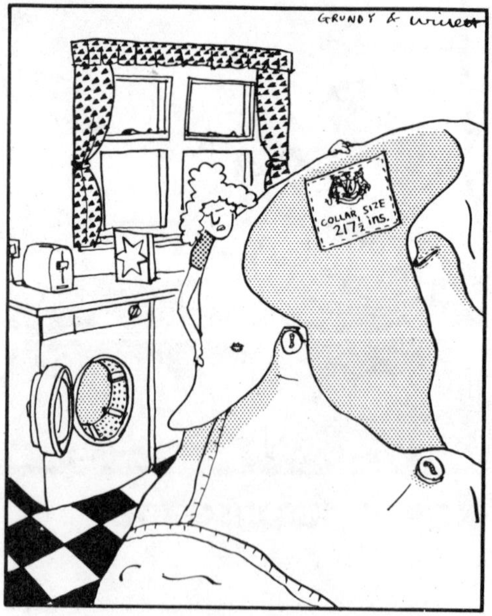
GRUNDY & WILLETT
COLLAR SIZE 217½ ins.

Lipstick on King Kong's collar.

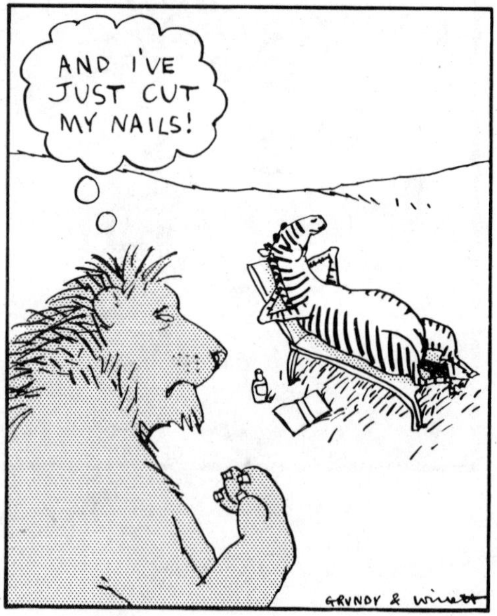
AND I'VE JUST CUT MY NAILS!
GRUNDY & WILLETT

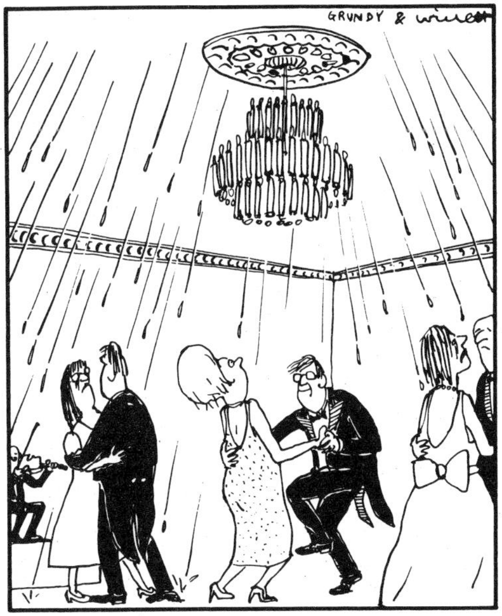
GRUNDY & WILLETT
Unfortunately, Harry's fancy footwork turned out to be an ancient rain dance.

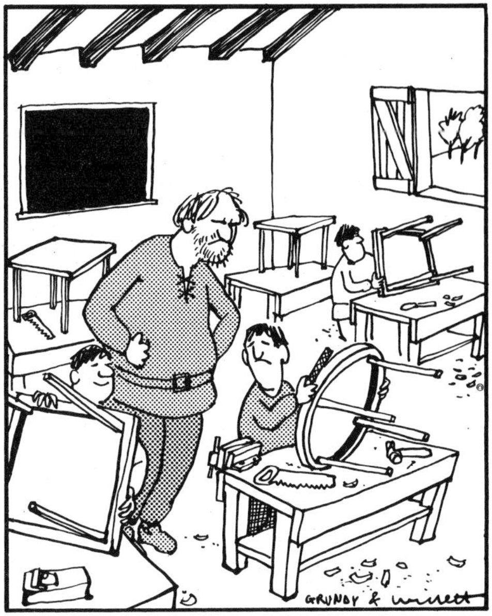
GRUNDY & WILLETT
Young King Arthur in woodworking class.

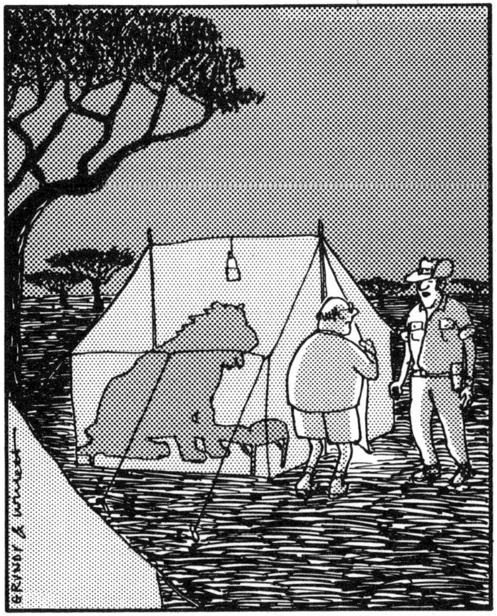
GRUNDY & WILLETT
"Now don't forget, check for spiders and snakes."

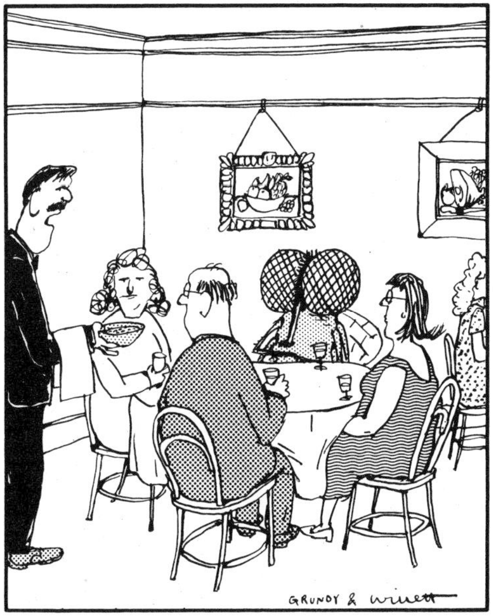
GRUNDY & WILLETT
"OK, who ordered the soup?"

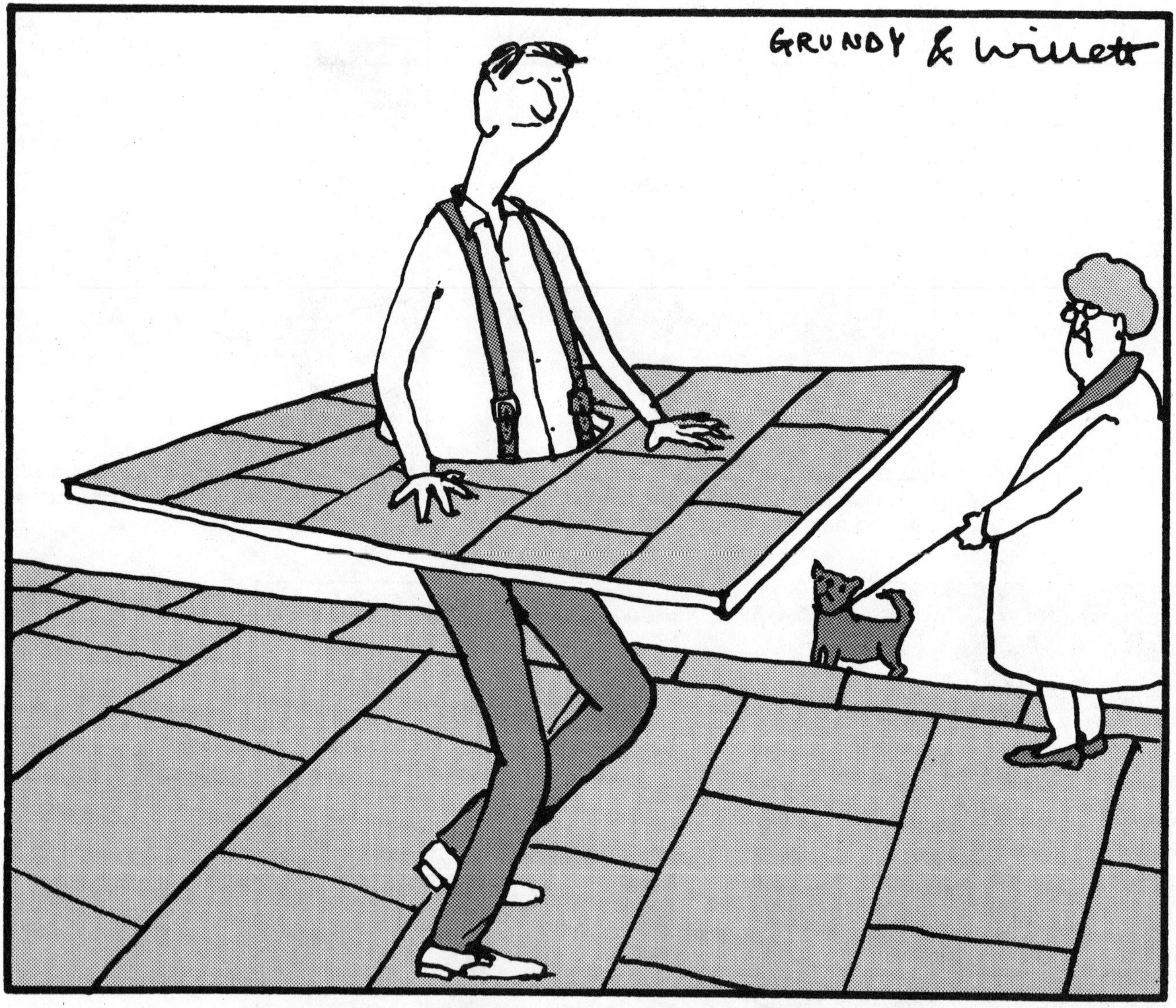
GRUNDY & Willett

Herman overcomes his fear of heights.

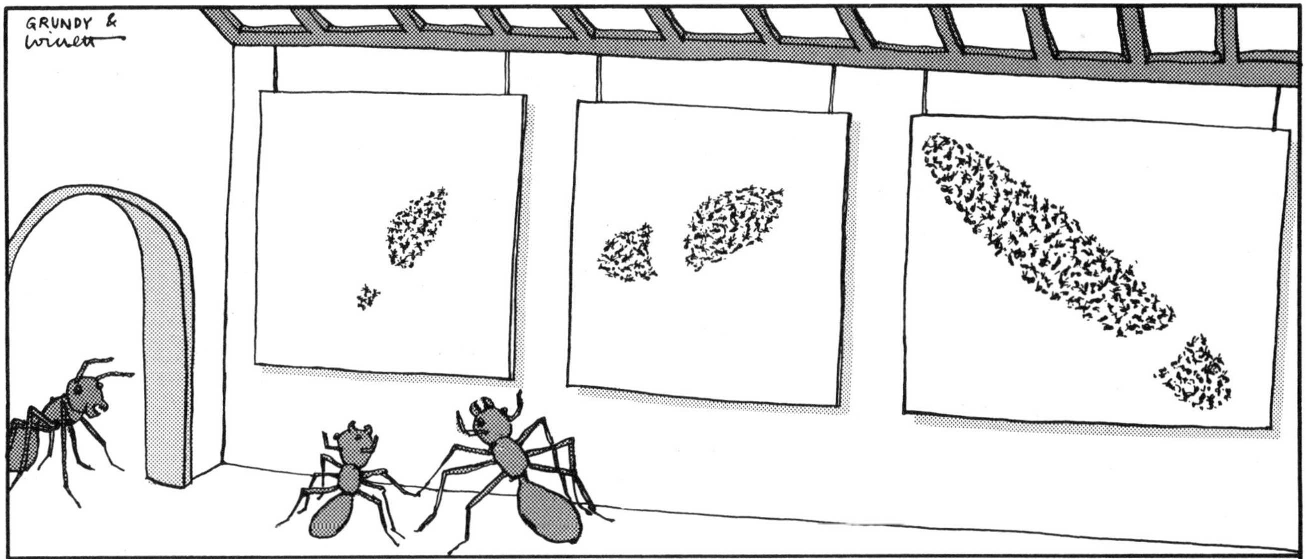
GRUNDY &
Willett

Great disasters of the ant world.

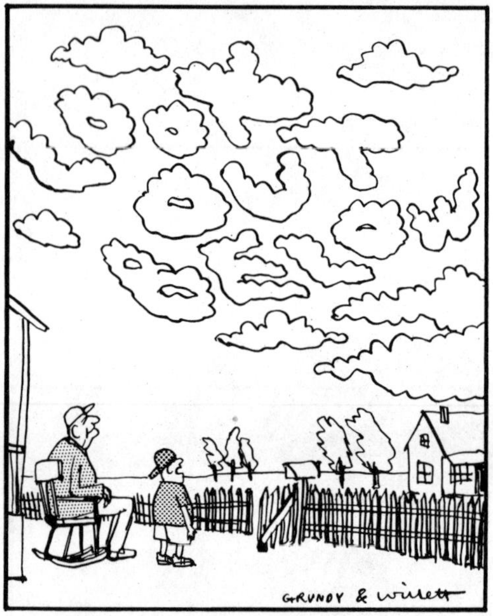

"Wow, Grandpa! Just by looking at the sky you can tell there's a storm coming!"

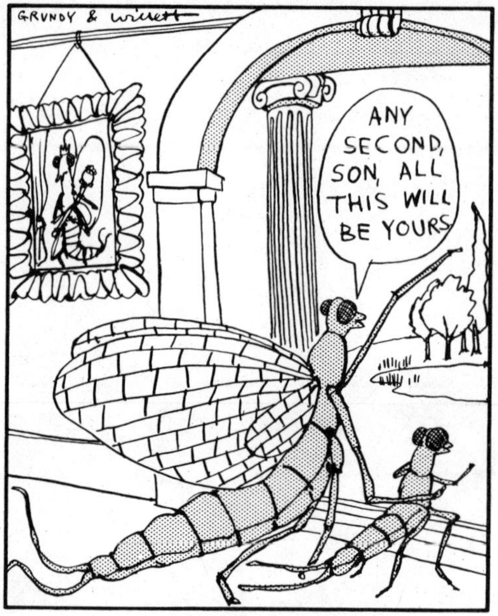
ANY SECOND, SON, ALL THIS WILL BE YOURS

Mayfly dynasty.

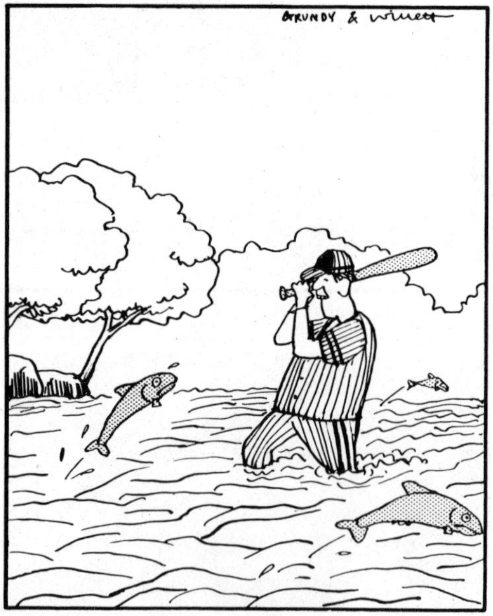

Batting practice.

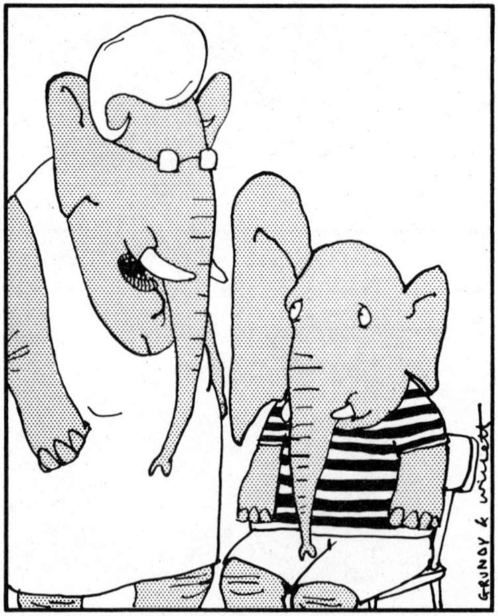

"Well, son, your dad was African."

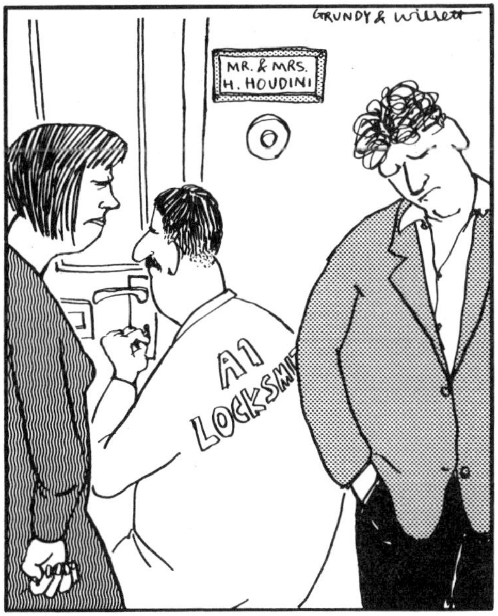
GRUNDY & WILLETT
MR. & MRS.
H. HOUDINI
A1
LOCKSMI

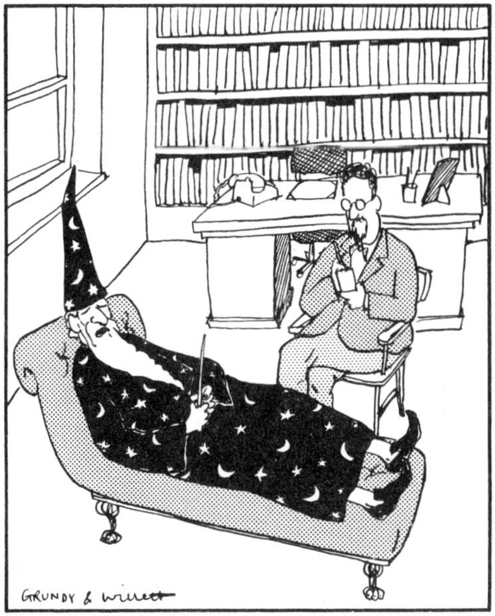
GRUNDY & WILLETT

"I'm a witch trapped in a wizard's body."

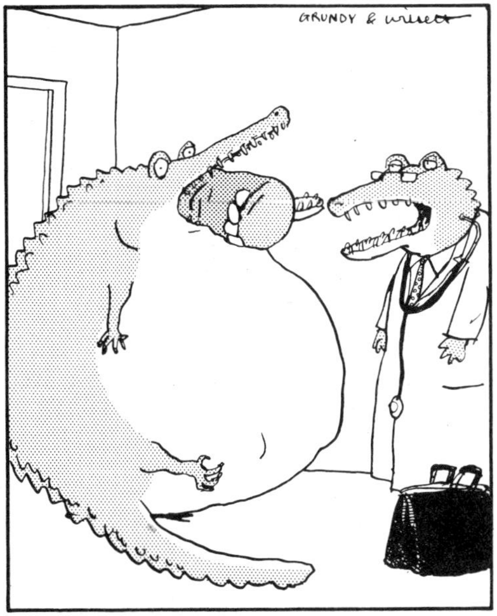
GRUNDY & WILLETT

"Classic case of biting off more than you can chew."

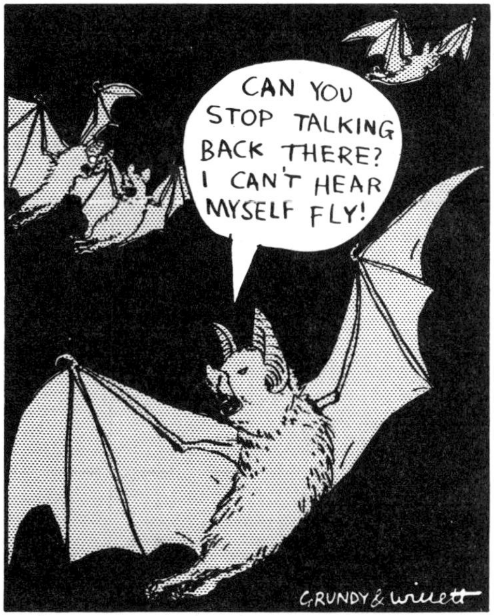
CAN YOU STOP TALKING BACK THERE? I CAN'T HEAR MYSELF FLY!
GRUNDY & WILLETT

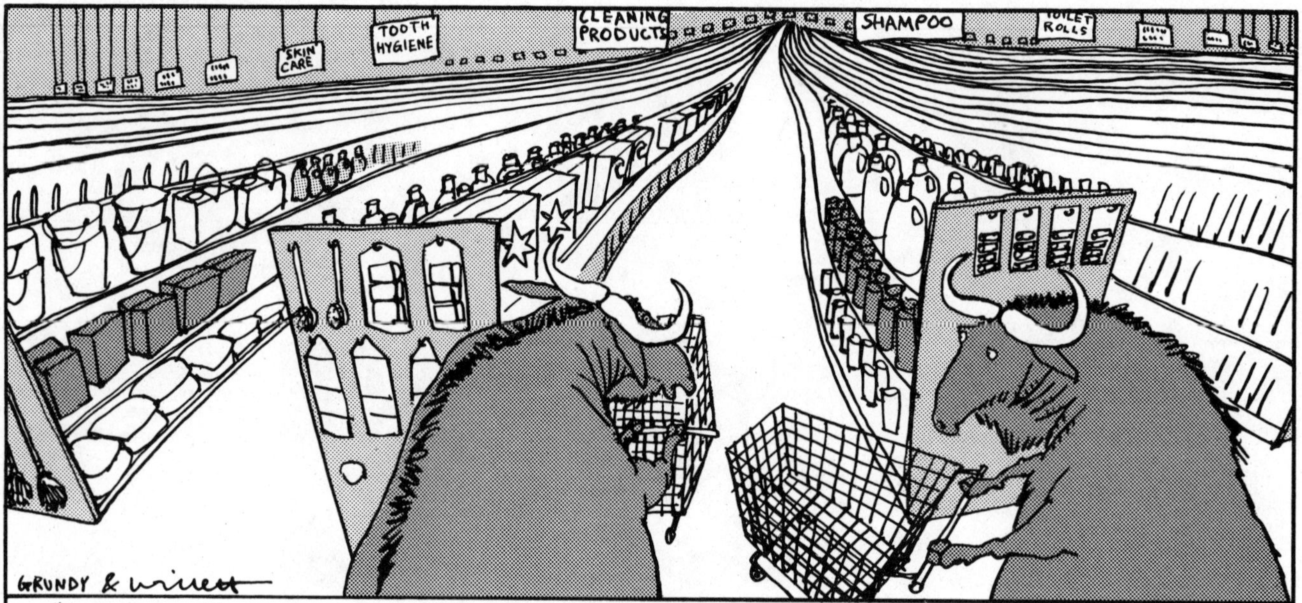
TOOTH HYGIENE
SKIN CARE
CLEANING PRODUCTS
SHAMPOO
TOILET ROLLS
GRUNDY & Willett
"Why is it, every dry season they move the darn food south?!"

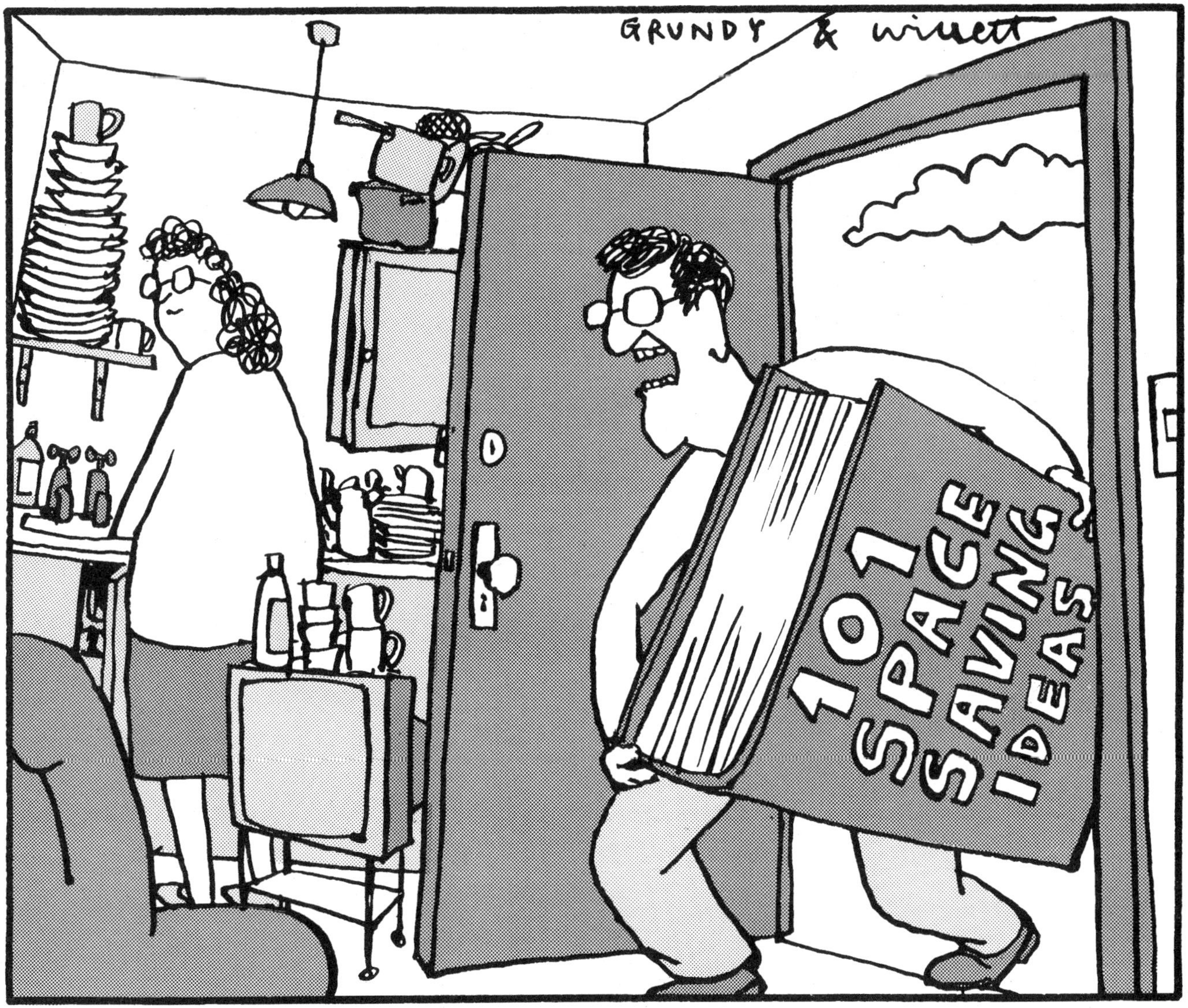
GRUNDY & Willett
101
SPACE
SAVING
IDEAS

"Honey, our problems are solved!"

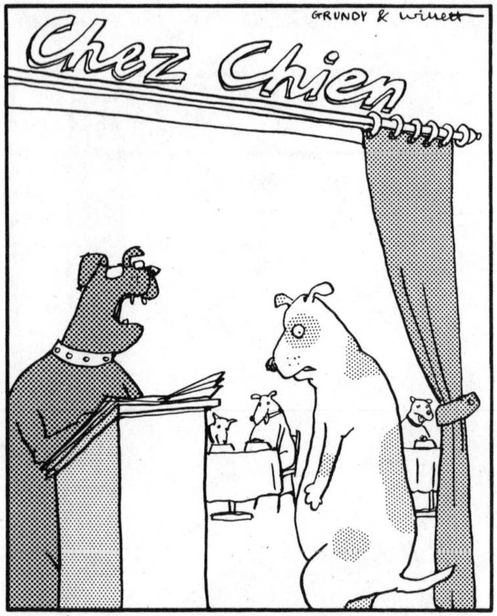
Chez Chien

"Sorry, sir, you're not allowed in without a collar."

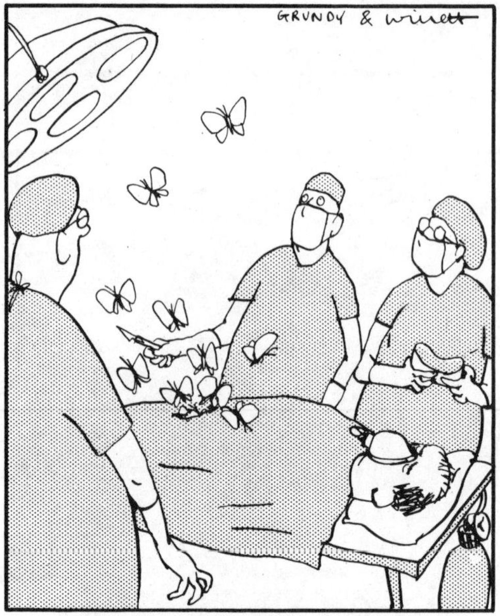

Surgeons discover the cause of Harold's nervous stomach.

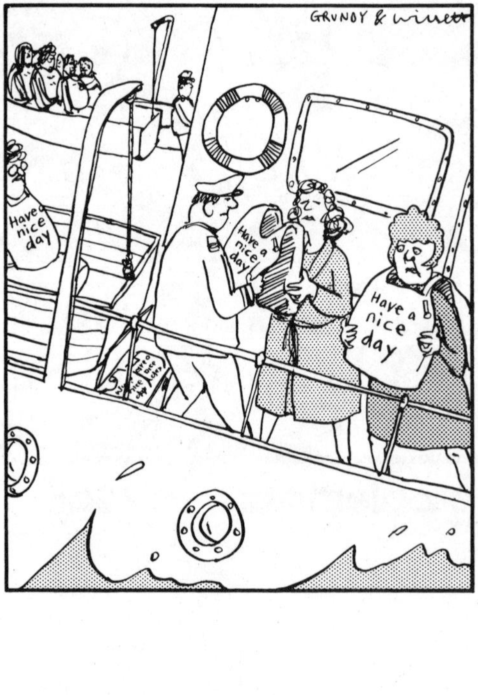
Have a nice day
Have a nice day
Have a nice day

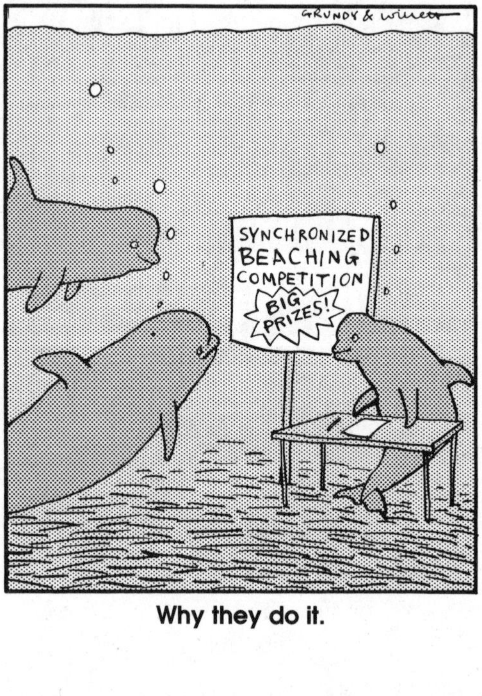
SYNCHRONIZED BEACHING COMPETITION
BIG PRIZES!

Why they do it.

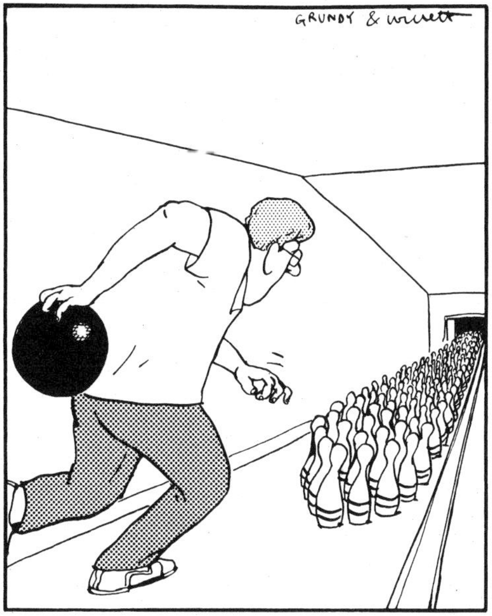
GRUNDY & Willett

Three hundred and ten-pin bowling.

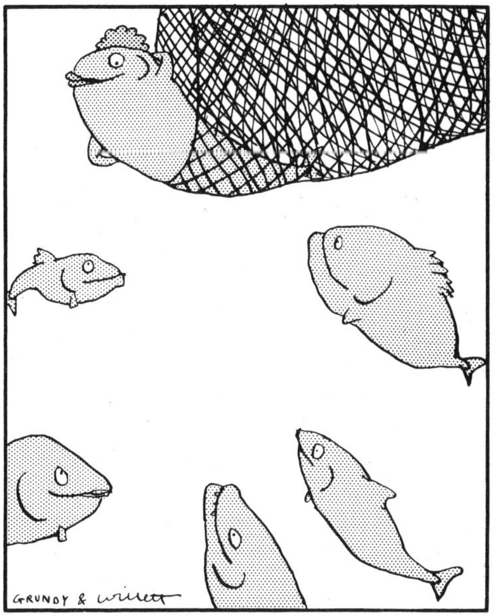
GRUNDY & Willett

Daphne looked great in fishnet.

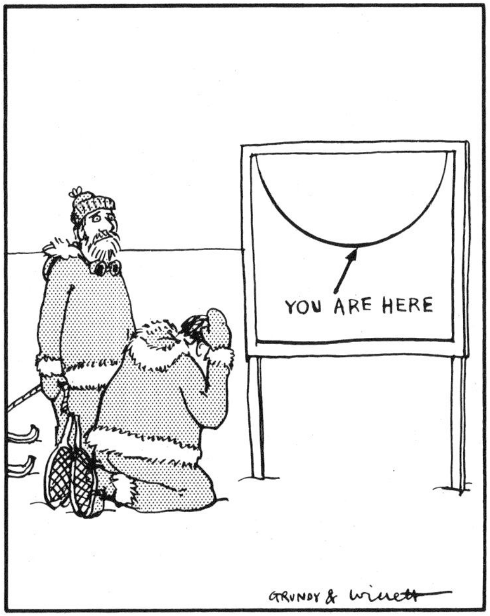
YOU ARE HERE
GRUNDY & Willett

1912: Captain Scott discovers he's not the first to reach the South Pole.

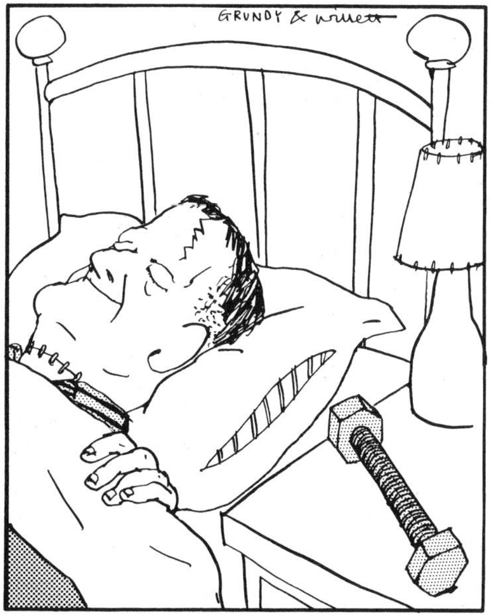
GRUNDY & Willett

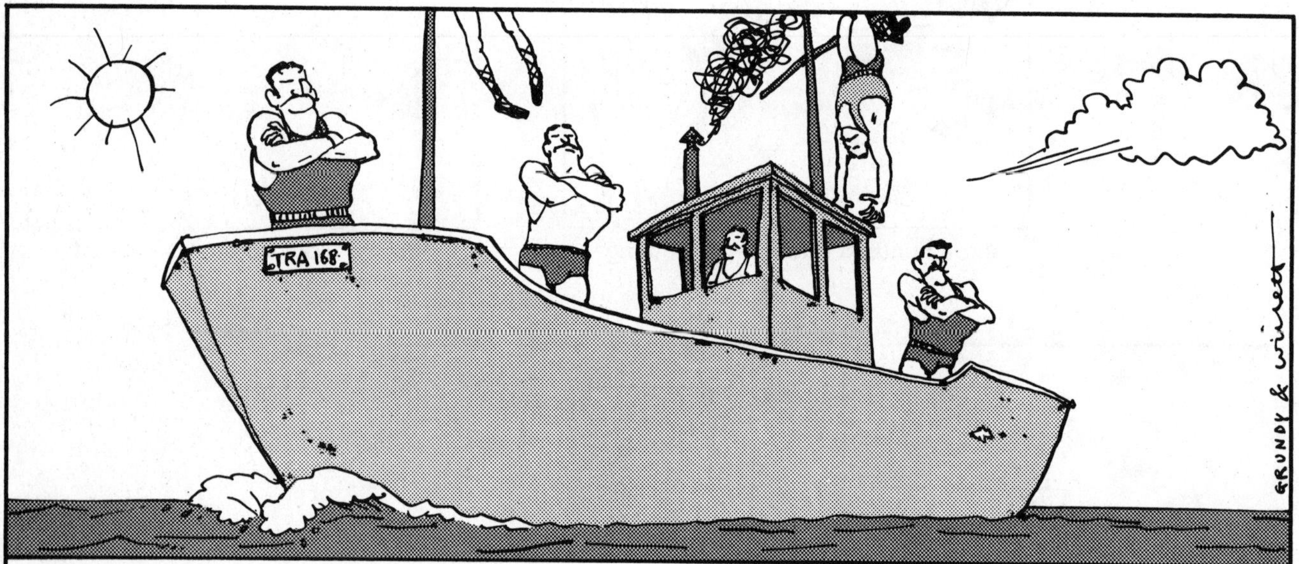
TRA 168
GRUNDY & WILLETT

After retiring from the circus, the Flying Blondinis never caught any fish, as they refused to use a net.